PIONEER EXPLORERS
of
INTELLIGENT DESIGN

PIONEER EXPLORERS *of* INTELLIGENT DESIGN

INTELLIGENT DESIGN

Scientists Who Made a Difference

DON B. DEYOUNG

BMH BOOKS
Winona Lake, Indiana
www.bmhbooks.com

Pioneer Explorers of Intelligent Design
Scientists Who Made a Difference

Copyright 2006 by Donald DeYoung

ISBN 10: 0-88469-073-3
ISBN 13: 978-0-88469-073-3
Inspiration/Motivation/Biography
INS/CHI/BIO

Cover and page design by Terry Julien

BMH Books
P.O. Box 544, Winona Lake, IN 46590
www.bmhbooks.com

Printed in the United States of America

TABLE *of* CONTENTS

Vesalius, Andreas
Waksman, Selman Abraham

Ampere, André-Marie
Bacon, Roger
Berkeley, George
Biot, Jean-Baptiste
Clarke, Samuel
Colding, Ludvig August
Compton, Arthur
Daniels, Farrington
Foucault, Jean
Fownes, George
Franklin, Benjamin
Gladstone, John
Grosseteste, Robert
Haak, Theodore
Helmont, Johannes Baptista van
Hess, Victor
Keill, John
Malebranche, Nicolas
Meitner, Lise
Mendeléev, Dmitri
Millikan, Robert
Moray, Robert
Morley, Edward
Morris, Henry
Newcomen, Thomas
Oersted, Hans Christian
Planck, Max
Priestley, Joseph
Schiff, Leonard Isaac
Sprat, Thomas
Tilloch, Alexander
Ure, Andrew
Volta, Alessandro

FOREWORD

My friend and co-author of *Our Created Moon* (2004), Dr. Don DeYoung, has provided for us an illuminating and encouraging "Hebrews 11 Hall of Fame" for creation science. These 144 major contributors to scientific discovery during the past 500 years believed in the God of creation and the biblical record of His mighty works. This alone puts to rest the persistent idea in most of the academic world (including my own alma mater, Princeton University) that science is at its best when biblical creationism is totally excluded.

Our Lord Jesus Christ, through whom "all things were created" (Colossians 1:16), insisted that the creation record in Genesis be interpreted literally (cf. Matthew 18:4). And through the centuries this has encouraged many of God's servants to view the heavens and the earth through the lens of infallible Scripture.

The author of the book of Hebrews appeals to a great "cloud of witnesses" in the Old Testament who *believed* the Word of God; sixteen of whom are specifically named. These people of faith are still "surrounding us" and motivating us also to "lay aside every encumbrance, and the sin which so easily entangles us," so that we may "run with endurance the race that is set before us fixing our eyes on Jesus, author and perfecter of faith" (Hebrews 12:1-2).

In God's gracious providence, may we become part of a new "cloud of witnesses" to the truth of His written Word, to encourage a new generation of scientists to run the race of faith for the glory of God!

John C. Whitcomb, Th. D.
Indianapolis, Indiana

INTRODUCTION

It is often assumed that modern science and biblical creation are in direct conflict. How can one properly explore nature with an open mind if God is assumed to be the originator and sustainer of all things? Does not such a religious bias disqualify one as a scientist? The 144 short biographies included in this book provide a convincing answer: A biblical foundation actually encourages scientific inquiry and understanding. The entire foundation of modern science and technology was laid down by men and women of faith. Their biblical worldview was not a hindrance to achievement, but instead motivated them to outstanding accomplishments.

In 1982 Henry Morris wrote a small book titled *Men of Science, Men of God*. It demonstrated that scholarship and Christianity are entirely compatible by describing the biblical background of more than 100 pioneer scientists. Their names are listed in the Appendix of this book. *Men of Science* has been a great encouragement to Christians who are bombarded with secular trends in science. There is a rich biblical heritage to nature study, now nearly forgotten.

This new volume builds on the same theme by presenting the testimonies of many additional men and women who were leaders in science, exploration, mathematics, and medicine. Some of these pioneers may be unfamiliar today but during their lifetimes most were household names.

Several criteria were used in the selection of entries for this volume. First, each person made significant contributions to our understanding of how creation works. Second, their religious worldviews and testimonies were well known, to the extent that a personal faith often is mentioned in modern secular biographical works. Not all of the included names necessarily represent the young-earth view of creation, but the demonstrations of solid biblical faith are without question. Third, an effort was made to document personal beliefs with direct quotes whenever possible. The entries are limited to deceased persons so that an overview of entire lifetimes is available.

Many science pioneers distinguished themselves in several fields. Thus the particular category selected for each name is somewhat arbitrary. There are also some uncertainties in name spellings and dates. The book chapters cover the topics of astronomy, earth science, exploration, life science, mathematics, medical science, and physical science. Names within each chapter are placed in alphabetical order. There is also a final chapter titled "Missing Persons" which describes several major scientists who were especially antagonistic to the theistic worldview. These individuals unfortunately are missing from the long list of positive testimonies. Sources are listed at the end of the book for further study and documentation. Unless specified otherwise, quotations are taken from the *Dictionary of Scientific Biography* (Gillispie, 1070).

In 1998, one thousand randomly selected scientists were surveyed as to their belief in God (Larson and Witham, 1999). The results were surprising to many: 40 percent expressed faith in a personal God with confident belief in an afterlife. A similar survey 84 years earlier, in 1914, gave nearly the same percentage for belief in the Creator. Clearly, those who predict the imminent demise of Christianity in today's high-tech world are wrong. Biblical faith has always been important to many researchers for their proper scientific understanding of nature.

The same 1998 survey was also given to the select scientists who are members of the U.S. National Academy of Science (NAS). Congress founded this elite group of about 1,800 members in 1863 to advise the government on important matters of science, engineering, and medicine. Many of the members are university leaders and Nobel Prize winners. On the survey, more than 90 percent of these men and women categorized themselves as atheistic or agnostic on religious matters. In the NAS there appears to be a dramatic contrast between scientific expertise and a lack of basic wisdom concerning the God of the universe. It is the influence of this group that largely controls U.S. research spending, public education, and the media. The NAS elects its own members so there is little hope for change anytime soon. The following chapters describe equally gifted scientific leaders from the past who readily acknowledged their Creator. May their testimonies be an encouragement to you. And may the lives of faith briefly described in this book inspire the next generation of science leaders.

Chapter 1

ASTRONOMY

Astronomy is one of the earliest science disciplines. Since the time of Adam and Eve, stargazers have looked upward at the night sky in reverence and wonder. Astronomers work with vast distances measured in millions or billions of light years. A single light year represents about six trillion miles, or twelve million round trips to the moon. Telescopes reveal stars as numerous as the sand grains on all the world's seashores. One might conclude that astronomy teaches humility above other nature studies. This was indeed true for the pioneer astronomers included here.

James Bradley (1693-1762) was an ordained British pastor. He also held great interest in astronomy and was a friend of Edmund Halley, famous for his comet studies. Bradley's stargazing activity resulted in many important discoveries. He mounted a vertical telescope in his aunt's basement and cut holes (with permission!) through the floors and ceiling. Careful observation of the particular star called Gamma Draconis during 1728 revealed the *aberration* of starlight. Aberration is a small angular slant shown by incoming starlight because of the earth's revolution around the sun. It is similar to the way raindrops appear to strike the windshield of a moving car. Bradley also discovered the slight *nutation*, or wobble, of the earth's rotation axis because of the gravitational pull of the sun and moon. Bradley held Britain's respected position called *Astronomer Royal* for 20 years. One of his projects was the compilation of a star catalog with exact positions measured for 60,000 stars. This catalog remains useful today, three centuries later. Bradley was a benevolent man, a faithful husband and father, and he displayed a strong faith in the Creator of the universe.

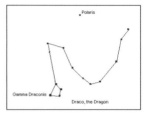

James Bradley studied the star Gamma Draconis. This star is visible in the northern sky near Polaris, the North Star.

Arthur Eddington explored the interior properties of distant stars.

Arthur Eddington (1882-1944) was trained in astronomy at the British Royal Observatory in Greenwich, England. He pioneered research in the physics of stars with an emphasis on stellar interiors. Eddington was the first to calculate the diameter of red giant stars, later verified with telescopes. These impressive stars are 10-100 times larger than our sun. In 1919 Eddington traveled to the southern hemisphere and measured the slight bending of starlight near the sun during an eclipse. This verified details of Einstein's general relativity theory. Eddington grew up in a Quaker home and maintained a strong pietistic faith all his life. Pietism combines conservative biblical doctrine, reverence for God, and an active Christian commitment. In his publications Eddington taught that Creation details merited being measured, explored, and appreciated. In *Science and the Unseen World* (1929), he declared that the meaning of life was to be found in spiritual reality rather than in science data alone. He believed that the spiritual realm was just as real as the world of nature. Eddington wrote, "You will understand the true spirit neither of science nor of religion unless seeking is placed at the forefront." He scoffed at detailed philosophical proofs, whether for or against God's existence. He concluded, "The most flawless proof of the existence of God is no substitute for [our relationship with Him]; and if we have that relationship, the most convincing disproof is turned harmlessly aside."

David Fabricius (1564-1617) was a German astronomer who discovered the first known variable star, one that shows a changing pattern of brightness. This star was later named Mira, pronounced "Myra," Latin for wonderful or marvelous. Mira is located in the December constellation Cetus, which is pictured as a whale or a sea serpent. Fabricius observed the light output of Mira slowly changing during the year 1596. Today Mira is thought to expand and contract over a 331 day period somewhat like a soap bubble, resulting in its changing light output. The star is called a *supergiant* and is more than 400 times larger than the sun. By observing sunspots, David Fabricius and his son Johannes also measured the rotation time for the sun, 25-35 days. Fabricius had friendships with both astronomers Tycho Brahe and Johann Kepler. He also was the minister of a local Dutch Reformed church. Faith in God and preaching duties held first place in Fabricius' life. Astronomy was a secondary interest in which the Lord blessed Fabricius with several discoveries including the star Mira.

James Ferguson (1710-1776) was a Scottish astronomer and instrument maker. At an early age he taught himself to read and write. His interest in astronomy was kindled while tending sheep through many evenings. Ferguson published technical papers concerning solar eclipses, and he

Scottish astronomer James Ferguson.

also constructed theoretical models for the formation of the planets. Ferguson wandered somewhat from the truth of direct supernatural creation. He promoted the nebular hypothesis whereby the planets formed slowly from collapsing gas clouds. However, unlike the philosophers of his day, including Immanuel Kant and Pierre Simon Laplace, Ferguson gave God full credit for giving all matter its properties at the moment of Creation. Ferguson rejected a random, chance beginning for the solar system. He realized that the complexity of space objects provides strong evidences of supernatural creation.

Pierre Gassendi (1592-1655) was a personal friend of the famous astronomer Galileo. Gassendi was the first observer to watch a planetary transit of the sun, that of Mercury in 1631. During this unusual event the planet passes directly in front of the sun and appears as a tiny black dot moving slowly across the solar surface. This particular observation helped verify Kepler's laws of planetary motion.

Mercury moving across the face of the sun in 2003. The planet images are 15 minutes apart (NASA/ESA).

Gassendi also experimented with the principle of inertia and helped verify this universal tendency of objects either to remain at rest or in constant motion. He also introduced the term *aurora borealis*, or "northern dawn," in 1621 to describe the northern lights. Gassendi supported Galileo's heliocentric idea that God had directed the earth to revolve about the sun. He believed that God had created all the atoms of the universe in a single stroke, and correctly taught that the Creation was open to detailed analysis. It was the recognition of dependable, created laws in nature that made scientific inquiry possible. Gassendi also taught that man was given an immaterial soul, which made him a creature distinct from the animal world.

Caroline Herschel (1750-1848) lived in the shadow of two famous astronomers, her brother William and also her nephew John Herschel. William discovered the planet Uranus in 1781 while Caroline worked at his side as an astronomy assistant. She diligently taught herself the mathematical details of the heavens and soon began making her own observations. Caroline catalogued 14 new space objects including several gaseous nebulae and also what is today known as the Andromeda Galaxy. Between 1786-97 she discovered eight new comets, an outstanding accomplishment. The British Royal Astronomical Society voted Caroline a gold medal in 1828 and later made her an honorary member. She lived until age 98 and continued astronomy research to the end. All her life Caroline Herschel displayed a strong Christian testimony. She composed her own epitaph, which appears on her grave in Hanover, Germany:

Caroline Herschel distinguished herself in both music and astronomy. She discovered many comets and gas clouds in space.

> *Here lies the earthly veil of Caroline Herschel.*
> *Born in Hanover, March 16, 1750*
> *The eyes of her who passed to glory,*
> *While below turned to the starry heavens…*
> *[She followed] to a better life her father, Isaac Herschel.*

Bartholomew Keckermann (1571-1609)

was a Polish leader in astronomy, mathematics, and educational philosophy. He had a special interest in the nature and origin of comets. Halley's Comet made its appearance toward the end of his life, in 1607. At this early stage of astronomy understanding, Keckermann taught that comets were a heavenly sign of God's wrath and impending judgment. According to Revelation 8:10-12 and elsewhere, there will indeed be multiple signs in the heavens in the last days. Keckermann also did research in navigation, optics, and geography. Keckermann held to a Calvinist faith in the Creator.

Halley's Comet was studied by Bartholomew Keckerman in 1607. This comet returns every 75-76 years. Its next visit is 2061.

Henrietta Swan Leavitt (1868-1921) spent her childhood in Ohio. Her interest in astronomy began during studies at what is now Radcliffe College in Cambridge, Massachusetts. This eventually led to her life's work at the Harvard

College Observatory in Cambridge. She discovered four novae or exploding stars, and also cataloged more than 2,400

variable stars. Miss Leavitt had a special interest in the properties of Cepheid variable stars. These important stars reveal their distance from earth by the way their light output changes over time. She helped calibrate this distance method, thus providing an important yardstick for measuring the depths of space. Cepheid variable measurements remain today a popular technique for determining

Overcoming deafness and gender bias, Henrietta Leavitt made major contributions to astronomy.

distances to remote stars and galaxies. Throughout her life Henrietta Leavitt remained loyal to her pastor father and also to her Puritan roots. Biographer Solon Bailey describes her as "a devoted member of her immediate family circle...unselfishly considerate in her friendships, steadfastly loyal to her principles and deeply conscientious and sincere in her Christian life and character" (Bailey, 1922).

Maria Mitchell (1818-1889) was the first noted woman astronomer in North America. She was also the first woman invited to join the American Academy of Science. Her discovery of Comet Mitchell in 1847 called attention to the important role of American women in science. She was educated chiefly by her father, and then enjoyed a distinguished career as an astronomy professor at Vassar College in Poughkeepsie, New York. All her life Maria presented a

Maria Mitchell was the first noted woman astronomer in America (1851 painting by Herminia Dassel).

strong testimony to the Creator. She wrote, "Every formula which expresses a law of nature is a hymn of praise to God." Her diary further states that "There is a God and He is good...I try to increase my trust in this, my only article or creed" (Gormley, 1995). At her birthplace in Nantucket, Massachusetts, the Maria Mitchell Association was founded in 1902. In her honor it maintains an observatory, library, and science museum.

Gottfried Wendelin (Godefroy Vendelin, 1580-1667) was a leading Flemish astronomer of his era. He bravely promoted the heliocentric view, which states that the earth circles the sun. This was at a time when persecution or death could result from such thinking that opposed geocentricism. Wendelin showed in 1626 that the satellites or moons of Jupiter exactly followed Kepler's recently discovered laws of motion. Isaac Newton later credited Wendelin in his classic book *Principia* (1687) for contributing to Newton's understanding of nature. Wendelin was an ordained priest in Brussels and held a deep Catholic faith in the Creator.

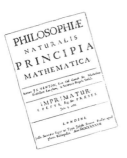

Gottfried Wendelin contributed ideas to Isaac Newton's 1687 book Principia which gave rise to modern physical science.

Thomas Wright (1711-1786) studied astronomy in eighteenth century England. He first proposed the disk-shaped model for the Milky Way Galaxy. Wright also correctly taught that the universe was made up of countless other galaxies. In a book called *An Original Theory* (1750), he speculated about other vast star systems beyond our own galaxy. It was not until almost two centuries later, in 1925, that Edwin Hubble observed these distant galaxies using the 100-inch Mount Wilson telescope in California. Thomas Wright was far ahead of his time in realizing the great size of the universe. He also worked diligently to integrate scientific observations with biblical theology. While the telescope could show the structure of the universe, Wright taught that religion alone provided a proper understanding of nature. In one of Wright's early models, God's abode was placed at the physical center of the universe with the far-distant outer darkness of space as a place of eternal punishment.

An artist's drawing of the Milky Way. There are 100 billion known galaxies in the universe (NASA).

Chapter 2

EARTH SCIENCE

Earth Science concerns volcanoes, earthquakes, seafloor spreading, waterfalls, dinosaur fossils, beautiful gemstones, and much more. These certainly are not dry, dusty topics! The biblical foundation of geology, once dominant in universities worldwide, is now nearly forgotten. However, the pioneer geologists of this chapter displayed strong creation testimonies during their successful careers in research and teaching.

Georgius Agricola (1494-1555), also known as **George Bauer,** spent his life improving the health and welfare of miners throughout Europe. By day and night he visited the mines and smelting houses to observe work conditions. Already in Agricola's day there were spirited environmental debates over mining operations. Agricola based his support for this industry on three biblical points. First, he believed the earth was given to mankind to manage and cultivate according to Genesis 2:15, including the mineral resources. Second, metals from the earth are used in products that enrich life and preserve health as God intended. Third, all God's gifts are good, including the earth's abundant natural resources. Agricola's book *De re metallica* ("On Metallurgy," 1556) was a masterpiece of pioneer technical writing in geology. He was one of the first to classify minerals according to their color, density, and texture. Agricola is considered the father of modern mineralogy, and his publications were widely used by geologists for more than 200 years. Agricola also coined the word *fossil* in 1546, today describing any permanent record of life from the past.

(Top image) German Scholar Georgius Agricola is known as the father of mineralogy. (Bottom image) Mining operations drawn by Georgius Agricola in 1556.

Louis Bourguet (Bourget, 1678-1742) was a Swiss naturalist with a special interest in mineralogy. He was the first to classify minerals into clays, stones, metals, and other subdivisions. One of Bourguet's technical papers in 1729 made the clear distinction between organic and inorganic (living and nonliving) growth. He also studied stalactites in caves and described their internal radial crystal structure. Bourguet saw crystal organization and other patterns in nature as coming from the direct plan of God. He also believed that the world's present topography or surface features were largely due to the effects of the Genesis Flood. Bourguet owned a collection of Bible translations in 50 languages and is said to have read them all. He was truly a student of the earth and also of God's Word.

Parker Cleaveland (1780-1858) authored *An Elementary Treatise on Mineralogy and Geology* in 1816, the first important mineralogical text published in the United States. Cleaveland graduated from Harvard College and spent a lifetime exploring the mineral resources of North America. A descendant of Puritan settlers, Cleaveland held to a conservative Christian faith and he opposed the teaching of any geological theory that disagreed with the biblical account of creation. His public testimony did not diminish teaching invitations that he received from almost every major American college during his career. He was renowned for his exciting classroom demonstrations. Cleaveland's career was spent at Bowdoin College in Brunswick, Maine, where today one can tour Cleaveland Chemistry Hall, named in his honor.

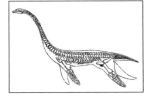

William Conybeare (1787-1857) was a British geologist with expertise in fossil identification. He wrote the first description of a plesiosaur fossil in *Translations of the Geological Society of London* (1824). Paleontologist Mary Anning had discovered this fossil. The 40-foot marine reptile had a long neck and fearsome teeth. Conybeare concluded that the plesiosaur body was directly designed by the Creator for aquatic life. To Conybeare, the creature was an exquisite example of the orderliness and diversity within Creation. Conybeare also identified the Carboniferous Period of earth history, sometimes also called the age of coal. In the creation view, coal deposits result from compressed vegetation that grew in the pre-flood world. In addition to his scientific work, Conybeare also published much biblical material.

(Top image) A plesiosaur illustration drawn in 1863 (Project Gutenberg). (Bottom image) Painting of William Conybeare at age 65 by H. B. Woodward.

John Fleming (1758-1857) is regarded as Scotland's foremost zoologist and geologist. He was also licensed as a minister in the Church of Scotland. Fleming had a special interest in physical evidence for the Genesis Flood. He gave detailed descriptions of the initial stages of the Flood with overflowing rivers, bursting lakes, and vast uprisings of the sea. Fleming also supported Thomas Chalmers' idea of a pre-Adamic world, today called the Gap Theory. This approach unnecessarily complicates the Genesis creation narrative, but at least it strongly opposes theistic evolution and evolutionary naturalism.

Richard Kirwan (1733-1812) was a chemist who helped form the Irish Royalty Society. This organization continues today, two centuries later. An outstanding mineralogist and creationist, Kirwan objected strongly to fellow geologist James Hutton's attacks on the book of Genesis. Kirwan wrote *Geological Essays* in 1799, promoting a literal view of the biblical creation account.

Goddard Chapel (1892) at Tufts University in Massachusetts where geologist Alfred Church Lane taught (Tufts University Archives).

Alfred Church Lane (1863-1948) worked as state geologist in both Michigan and Massachusetts. During his career Lane published more than 1,000 technical papers on economics, geology, politics, and religion. He was a lifelong Congregationalist and served as a church deacon for many years. He also volunteered his time to the YMCA and Boy Scouts. A plaque in Lane's honor hangs in the Goddard Chapel at Tufts College in Medford, Massachusetts. It is inscribed with Lane's own words from many years earlier, "Science and religion aim to know, to share, and to spread the truth freely."

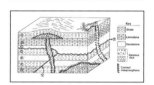

A modern geologic profile shows underground strata. Such profiles were first drawn by Johann Gottlab Lehmann in 1756.

Johann Gottlab Lehmann (1719-1767) was an early German geologist. He pioneered stratigraphy, the study of the order and sequence of sedimentary rock layers. Lehmann published the first geologic profile in 1756, illustrating the locations of underground rock layers. Lehmann firmly believed that the earth's fossil-bearing strata had originated during the Genesis Flood. He further suggested that the underlying, non-fossil-bearing rock, called Precambrian, was supernaturally formed during the creation week.

John Michell (1724-1793) was a prominent British geologist and astronomer. He is considered the father of seismology for his studies of the disastrous Lisbon, Portugal, earthquake of 1755. This was one of the most deadly earthquakes in history and was accompanied by a tsunami and fires. In 1760 Michell proposed that earthquake waves could be used to pinpoint exactly where an earthquake originated. His technique for locating an earthquake's *epicenter* is still used today. In astronomy Michell made the first realistic estimate of the distance to nearby stars. He also determined that many stars orbit others as binary systems. Gravity was not well understood in his day and Michell wrote concerning star associations, "Stars [are] placed nearly together, and [are] under the influence of some general law...or to some other appointment of the Creator." During his productive science career, Michell also found time for theological training. In his later years, while a member of the British Royal Society, Michell served faithfully as a local church pastor. Ministry activity seems to be quite common among pioneer scientists.

A copper engraving shows the destruction of Lisbon, Portugal in 1755. The earthquake was studied by British geologist John Michell.

Hugh Miller (1802-1859) was a self-taught geologist from Scotland. He wrote several books including an international bestseller about fossil fish titled *Footprints of the Creator* (1849). In this book Miller shows that the perfection and complexity of fish fossils disprove unplanned evolutionary development. Miller successfully combined his career in geology with an acceptance of biblical creation. He warned others that the popular evolutionary ideas of his time would lead eventually to atheism and immorality. A century and a half later his words ring true. Miller saw creation study as a refreshing and joyful alternative to the trends of secular science. He also emphasized the importance of seeing the work of Christ in the Creation. He asserted, "A [mere] belief in the existence of God is of as little ethical value as a belief in the existence

Geologist Hugh Miller studied fish fossils. Billions of such fossils reveal intricate design.

of the great sea-serpent." That is, one needs to recognize that God is personal and remains in control of this world. Miller's biographer, W.M. Mackenzie, wrote in 1905, "Probably no single man since has so powerfully moved the common mind of Scotland."

GENESIS 1:29

Five centuries ago, Bernard Palissy encouraged the decoration of gardens with Bible quotations.

Bernard Palissy (c. 1510-1590) was a French natural historian who excelled in the varied fields of agriculture, ceramics, and hydrology. Palissy gave the first description of wood petrification by minerals in ground water. In this process the wood is dissolved away and often is replaced by calcite or quartz. Palissy lectured widely concerning the natural world and often used fossils as object lessons. At the age of 36 Palissy converted to the Christian faith. From this point onward he actively integrated his new faith with scientific studies. As one example, in his lectures and agricultural writings, he described the ideal garden as one decorated both with flowers and also with biblical quotations. In following years the practice of placing scripture engravings in gardens became popular across Europe. At age 80, Palissy died while he was imprisoned for his faith at the Bastille in Paris.

Granville Penn (1761-1844) was an amateur geologist, one of the "Scriptural Geologists" of the 1800s. This was a group of clergymen and geologists in England who opposed the increasing denial of the global Genesis Flood. Penn defended biblical origins in his book titled *A Comparative Estimate of the Mineral and Mosaical Geologies* (1822). He wrote, "[Geology] not only conducts the intelligence…to the discernment of the God of nature, but advances it further to a distinct recognition of that God of nature in the God of Scripture."

Henry Sorby (1826-1908) was given a book at age 15 titled *Readings in Science*. It was published by the Society for Promoting Christian Knowledge, and this small book shaped Sorby's lifelong biblical view of nature. He was one of the first scientists to apply the microscope to geology and metallurgy. He also pioneered the use of polarizing filters to study thin rock sections and to identify minerals. Sorby came to be regarded as the father of microscope petrography. He was a loyal, conservative pillar of the Church of England. Sorby also belonged to London's Royal Society and was said to have little patience with those vocal members who were anti-religious.

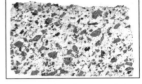

Henry Sorby pioneered the study of thin rock sections, which reveal details of minerals in rocks.

Peter Waage (1833-1900) was a Norwegian chemist and mineralogist. He discovered the chemical law of mass action that determines how proportions of elements combine to form compounds. Waage's Christian faith motivated his lifelong evangelistic work with youth. As one example he founded the Young Men's Christian Association (YMCA) in Norway. Waage also campaigned against liquor, having observed its negative impact on his fellow citizens of Norway.

Johan Gottschalk Wallerius (1709-1785) performed early chemistry and mineralogy experiments in Sweden. His work with soils led him to be called the father of agricultural chemistry. In his day Wallerius was an authority on the biblical account of the history of creation. He accepted fully the historical details of Genesis. At age 67 Wallerius wrote *Thoughts on the Creation* (1776), which was translated into many languages worldwide. In this book Wallerius gave full authority to the biblical account of creation, as opposed to natural theories of origin.

Johan Wallerius is known as the father of agricultural chemistry. The laboratory Wallerius built around 1750 still stands in Uppsala, Sweden.

George Frederick Wright (1838-1921), born in Ohio, was a founder of the Geological Society of America. Glacier studies took him to China, Greenland, and across North America. Wright promoted the idea of a single ice age that had taken place a few thousand years ago. He also believed that people were present during this ice age, an unpopular view in Wright's day. Many creationists would agree with Wright regarding the occurrence of a single, recent ice age. For 38 years Wright edited *Bibliotheca Sacra*, Latin for "Sacred Library." This is a major theological journal with continuous publication since 1843. It is carried on today by Dallas Theological Seminary. In his later years Wright championed the form of Darwinian theology called theistic evolution.

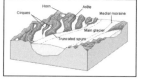

Glaciers were studied by American geologist George Wright. This drawing gives some glacier vocabulary.

Chapter 3

EXPLORATION

Most modern travelers enjoy airlines, near-instant communication, and comfortable lodging. In an earlier time, explorers who set out into the unknown needed great courage. There was extreme personal risk with no assurance of a safe return. Many were motivated by the biblical mandate of Genesis 1:28 to subdue the earth, that is, to explore, understand, and manage our world. The following individuals, representative of countless other pioneers, greatly succeeded in mapping the earth while honoring their Creator.

Isabella Bird Bishop explored remote lands and cultures 150 years ago. Her goals included sharing her faith and medicine with the world.

Isabella Bird Bishop (1832-1904) was the daughter of a British pastor. Well over a century ago, a strong urge to travel carried her to far parts of the world. In 1889 she set off for India where she founded several hospitals. Further missionary zeal carried Isabella to North America, the South Pacific, and across Asia. Along the way she braved the rapids of the Yangtze River in China and the snowstorms of Tibet. At this early time, travel was difficult and dangerous, especially for a single woman. Isabella wrote many popular books about her experiences with unfamiliar people, cultures, climates, and geography. For her efforts, Isabella was the first woman elected as a Fellow of Britain's Royal Geographic Society.

A replica of Christopher Columbus' flagship the Santa Maria. The original ship was about 60 feet long and carried 52 men.

Christopher Columbus (1451-1506) was the famous Italian explorer in the service of Spain. On August 3, 1492, he set out with a crew of 88 sailors aboard three ships, the *Nina*, the *Pinta*, and the *Santa Maria*. The goal was to reach Asia by sailing westward from Europe. Instead, however, the ships anchored 42 days later in the present-day Bahamas. Columbus was quick to give God credit for landfall. His journal reads, "God made me the messenger of the new heaven and the new earth...He showed me where to find it." Columbus later wrote a travel summary for King Ferdinand and Queen Isabella of Spain, "...maps were of [no] use to me: fully accomplished were the words of Isaiah." His reference was to Isaiah 11:10-12, which describes the reclaiming of distant, people "from the islands of the sea." Christopher Columbus firmly believed that his voyages were divinely guided. He took his first name, which means *Christ-bearer,* seriously. In later years Columbus completed three additional voyages across the Atlantic Ocean.

Robert FitzRoy (1805-1865) was captain of the HMS *Beagle* during the famous five-year world voyage, 1831-

1836, with Charles Darwin on board as chief naturalist. FitzRoy distinguished himself as a seaman,
explorer, meteorologist, cartographer, and later as
governor of New Zealand. FitzRoy wrote one of
the earliest textbooks on meteorology, *The Weather
Book* (1863). He completely rejected Charles Darwin's evolutionary ideas. One can only imagine the
conversations that took place aboard the *Beagle*
during their long journey together. In later years
FitzRoy pleaded unsuccessfully with his friend
Darwin to return to the biblical view of creation.

*Robert FitzRoy was captain
of the HMS Beagle during
Charles Darwin's voyage.
Fitzroy later was Governor
of New Zealand.*

Martin Frobisher (1535-1594) sailed under
the British flag during several unsuccessful efforts
to find a Northwest Passage across North America
to the Orient. In Canadian waters he discovered
Hudson Bay, and also what is today aptly called
Frobisher Bay. Seaman George Best who accompanied Frobisher wrote an account of their adventures
four centuries ago: "Many unknown lands and
islands [were] made known to us; Christ's name
spread; the gospel preached; infidels were converted to Christianity in places where before the name
of God had not once been heard of." Concerning
Frobisher's fleet of ships, George Best wrote that
any vessel approaching at night was suspected of
piracy and was hailed with these words, "Before the
world was God." If the challenged vessel belonged
to their fleet, the reply was, "After God came Christ
his Son." Navigator Martin Frobisher stated that he
was motivated by the lofty goal of exploring God's
worldwide creation. This goal is somewhat dimin-
ished by Frobisher's reputation of piracy, robbing
Spanish ships at sea during this frontier era.

*(Top image) Painting of
explorer Martin Frobisher
by Cornelis Ketal. (Bottom
image) Frobisher Bay was
discovered in 1576 during
efforts to find a northwest
passage across North
America to the Orient.*

John Harrison (1693-1776) solved one of the
greatest problems in world exploration without
ever leaving home. This British inventor made it
possible to sail the seas with accurate knowledge of

one's longitude. Voyagers at this time could easily determine their latitude, the distance above or below the equator, by observing stars. Longitude, however, the east-west position, was a far greater challenge with serious consequences. In 1707 during heavily overcast weather, 2,000 British sailors

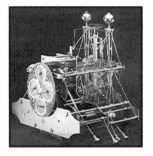

British inventor John Harrison's accurate clocks made seafaring safe.

perished when their fleet ran aground off England's southwest coast, a result of not knowing their longitude. This disaster led the British government to offer a large prize for anyone who could devise a simple method for determining one's longitude. John Harrison realized that the missing ingredient was an accurate shipboard clock. In the following years he constructed a series of virtually friction-free clocks. They needed no lubrication and did not rust or lose time aboard storm-tossed ships. These marine chronometers used gears and balance wheels instead of the then-common pendulum movement. Harrison's first clock, called H1 and completed in 1735, still ticks in the Maritime Museum in Greenwich, England. Forty years passed before Harrison's success was recognized and his clocks were utilized world-wide to save countless lives at sea. This solution of the longitude problem also was essential to the expansion of the British Empire. During his tireless efforts of clock development and final acceptance, Harrison maintained a Christian testimony. In 1759, upon receipt of the long-awaited longitude prize he said, "...there is neither any other mechanical or mathematical thing in the world that is more beautiful or curious in texture than this my watch...and I heartily thank Almighty God that I have lived so long, as in some measure to complete it." John Harrison's story was popularized in the 1995 book *Longitude* written by Dova Sobel, and the story was also made into a movie.

David Livingstone (1813-1873) arrived in Africa from Scotland in 1841, sent by the London Missionary Society. At great personal risk, Livingstone brought the gospel to Africa's unknown interior. He pushed 1,000 miles into the wilderness, seeking a route or "missionary road" for fellow missionaries to travel. Livingstone saw the pressing need to improve African economic conditions and he also worked to abolish the slave trade. His wife and child died in Africa, and Livingstone suffered greatly from malaria. He probably would not have called himself an explorer but the title is well deserved. Livingstone was the first outsider to map the great Zambezi River of East Africa. He also discovered Victoria Falls and Lake Nyasa. His journals are filled with scientific and geographic details that helped outsiders understand the African continent. Livingstone's dedication to evangelism has inspired many other missionaries to this day. On Livingstone's tomb in Westminster Abbey, London, is the text John 10:16, "Other sheep I have which are not of this fold; them also I must bring."

Ferdinand Magellan (1480-1521) was the first explorer to circumnavigate the globe, in 1519. By this success Magellan correctly challenged certain religious authorities who taught a flat earth. Magellan wrote, "The Church says that the earth is flat, but I know it is round, for I have seen the shadow on the moon, and have more faith in a shadow than in the Church." On all his voyages Magellan carried a fervent missionary zeal to convert newly discovered ethnic groups to Christianity. One example was Magellan's preaching of the gospel to natives around the Philippine province of Cebu. As a result, the people of these islands today number millions of conservative Catholics. Hostile natives killed Portuguese navigator Magellan later in the Philippines, at age 41. In England's Oxford University library is a chair made from timber salvaged from Magellan's ship. Poet Abraham Cowley (1618-1667) honored Magellan with these words, "For Lo! A Seate of endless Rest is giv'n/ To her in Oxford, and to him in Heav'n."

David Livingstone was a Scottish explorer, doctor and missionary to Africa. He helped open the heart of Africa to the gospel.

Marco Polo (c. 1254-1324) is perhaps the greatest explorer, seaman, and cartographer the world has known. In 1271 this Italian wanderer began a 24-year journey throughout

Asia. His book *Travels of Marco Polo* (1298) became a geographic classic and was the only written account of the Far East available in Europe for the next five centuries. Marco

Polo maintained a personal Catholic faith during his long journeys. When he encountered Buddhism in China, he wrote about the Indian mystic Buddha, "Most certainly if he had been a Christian he would have been a great saint with Christ." Marco Polo also described Mount Ararat: "In the central part of Armenia stands an exceedingly large and high mountain, upon which, it is said, the ark of Noah rested, and for this reason it is termed the Mountain of the Ark." On his deathbed in Venice in 1324, Marco Polo freed his faithful servant with the words, "[Go free, and in the same way] may God absolve my soul from all guilt and sin."

An early painting shows explorer Marco Polo. He traveled throughout Asia seven centuries ago.

Ernest Shackleton (1874-1922) was a captain in the British Merchant Navy. In 1915 he led a bold expedition to Antarctica. Thirty volunteers traveled southward aboard the ship *Endurance*. The plan was to sail to the Antarctic region, and then be the first explorers to cross the icy continent on foot. Instead, however, the ship became trapped in sea ice and eventually was crushed. The men were completely out of touch with the world so no one knew of their desperate plight. Survival was at stake with the loss of the ship. Only the barest essentials could be kept as the men hiked across the ice to land and set up camp. By way of example, Shackleton held up the ship's Bible, tore out a single page, then laid the book on the ice. The passage he chose to keep included Job 38:29-30: "Out of whose womb came the ice? And the hoary frost of heaven, who hast gendered it? The waters are hid as with a stone, and the face of the deep is frozen" (King James Version). This symbolic event in a desperate situation showed Shackleton's familiarity and respect for Scripture. Shackleton and a small team later set out on an 800-mile crossing of the ocean in a small open lifeboat. They found help at a remote whaling station and all 30 men were eventually saved. This ended the twenty-month odyssey at the bottom of the world. It was later learned that one of Ernest Shackleton's men had secretly picked up the ship's Bible and kept it the entire time. Today it is on display in the archives of the Royal Geographical Society in London. One can read the inscription in the Bible that was originally presented to Shackleton by Britain's Queen Alexandra: "For the Crew of the *Endurance* from Alexandra, May 31, 1914. May the Lord help you do your duty and guide you through all dangers by land and sea. May you see the works of the Lord and all his wonders in the deep." One of Shackleton's later quotes summarized the expedition in verse: "We had seen God in His splendors, heard the text that Nature renders. We had reached the naked soul of man."

During the Antarctic voyage of Ernest Shackleton in 1915, the ship Endurance was crushed by ice. The entire crew of 30 men survived the ordeal (Royal Geographic Society).

Chapter 4

LIFE SCIENCE

Biologists are privileged to explore the world of plants, animals, and people. Today, evolution theory has permeated almost every aspect of modern life science. However, the pioneer biologists introduced in this chapter show that the creation worldview provides a strong basis for understanding our living world. The chapter also shows that botany, the study of plants, was of special interest in past centuries.

This portrait of Edgar Anderson is displayed in the Biology Library of Washington University, St. Louis.

Edgar Anderson (1897-1969) excelled in plant genetics. Two of his books were *Introgressive Hybridization* (1949) and *Plants, Man and Life* (1952), the latter book still popular. Living in Missouri, Anderson became a leading investigator of cross-breeding, or hybridization, as a source of variation within plant species. He introduced many new and improved plants to the midwest states from the Balkan countries, based on the similarity of their geographic climates. Anderson displayed a lifelong Christian faith and a strong desire to serve humanity. In later life he became an active member of the Quaker Church.

Saint Francis of Assisi (ca. 1181-1226) is known as the first ecologist. This discipline studies the interaction of living things with their environments. St. Francis spent many years in the Italian countryside exploring the details of creation in a wilderness sitting. He also wrote many poems and hymns of praise about the outdoors which are still instructive today, eight centuries later. The well-known hymn *All Creatures of Our God and King* contains the words and testimony of St. Francis. Verse five reads,

> *Let all things their Creator bless,*
> *And worship Him in humbleness.*
> *Praise the Father, praise the Son,*
> *And praise the Spirit, three in one.*

According to tradition, these words were written during a time of pain and loss for St. Francis. He

Painting of St. Francis of Assisi by El Greco.

had given all his possessions to the poor and he ministered to those afflicted with leprosy. His entire life was an expression of joyful thanks to God for the created world. St. Francis also wrote a challenge to live by example with these words, "Preach the Gospel always, and when necessary use words." A theologian as well as a pioneer naturalist, St. Francis founded the Franciscan religious order in A. D. 1209.

Henry Baker (1698-1774) was a British naturalist with many scientific interests. Publications of his microscope studies went through many editions. Baker made original investigations of different types of crystals. He regarded scientific instruments as a means to a deeper appreciation of God's creation. His 1742 book *The Microscope Made Easy* encouraged the public to explore creation on the small scale. Baker wrote, "Microscopes furnish us as it were with a new sense, unfold the amazing operations of Nature, and give mankind a deeper sense of 'the infinite Power, Wisdom, and Goodness of Nature's Almighty Parent.'" Microscopes and telescopes have indeed greatly expanded our appreciation of creation on the smallest and also the largest scales.

John Hutton Balfour (1808-1884) was a British physician with a special interest in botany studies. He became director of the Royal Botanical Gardens in London and also was professor of botany at Glasgow University in Scotland. Balfour was an outstanding teacher who authored several popular botany texts. A deeply religious Presbyterian, he saw in nature the clear confirmation of God's existence. Balfour authored significant books including *Plants of the Bible* (1857) and *Lessons from Bible Plants* (1870).

John Bartram (1699-1777) is known as the father of American botany. He was born in Pennsylvania and did early plant classification throughout the colonies. He introduced more than 100 American plant species into Europe. A friend of Benjamin Franklin, Bartram was the first to hybridize or interbreed flowering plants. He also organized the first American botanical garden in 1728. It continues today as *Bartram's Garden* in Philadelphia. At this garden site 250 years ago, John Bartram was stopped in his tracks by a daisy while plowing his fields. The beauty of this single flower inspired John and also his son to spend their lives exploring nature. Bartram traveled the eastern American wilderness from Canada to Florida. His entire life was spent as a Quaker with strong faith in his Creator. Bartram held the deistic view that God had started the universe, then let it operate

on its own. Above the front window of his house in 1770 he carved these words for all to see,
'Tis God alone, Almighty Lord,
The Holy One, by me ador'd.

William Bartram (1739-1823) followed in his father John's footsteps as a leading botanist and wildlife artist. William had great concern for the welfare of native American Indians and also for the suffering of animals. He described his research travels as "tracing and admiring the infinite power, majesty, and perfection of the great Almighty Creator." Bartram traveled through South Carolina, Georgia, and Florida making notes on animals and plants. The local Indians welcomed him with the name "Flower Hunter." His book *Travels* (1791) is a classic in the literature of North American exploration.

(Top image) William Bartram was a well-known American naturalist and writer. (Bottom image) The book Travels *(1791) by William Bartram showed high respect for American Indians.*

Stephen Hales (1677-1761) was a botanist, chemist, and Anglican clergyman. He became a leading English scientist as he pioneered experiments in plant and animal physiology. As one example, Hales explored transpiration, the loss of moisture from plant leaves. In 1727 he carefully measured the amount of water vapor given off by leaves, and verified that this is how plants regulate their temperature. Transpiration also plays a part in plant production of oxygen. Hales firmly believed in God's design of nature's details, and this faith provided the foundation for his scientific studies. He wrote, "The further researches we make into this admirable scene of things, the more beauty and harmony we see in them. And the stronger and clearer convictions they give us, of the being, power and wisdom of the divine Architect." Throughout Hales' science career he preached the gospel. In his own words, he believed that nature testified to the Creator "in framing for us so beautiful and well regulated a world."

David Hartley (1705-1757) was the son of a poor Anglican clergyman. David Hartley adopted the faith of his father and studied medicine. His book *Observations on Man* (1749) was the first published work in English to use the word "psychology" in its modern sense, the study of the mind and how it functions. Hartley wrote that man was able to discover order in nature chiefly because the human mind reflected the wisdom of God. David Hartley was a mentor and Christian example to the great chemist Joseph Priestley (1733-1804), who later discovered oxygen gas in the atmosphere. Like Hartley, Priestly also held a strong creationist belief.

David Hartley was a founder of modern psychology in England.

John Stevens Henslow (1796-1861) was professor of botany and geology at the University of Cambridge in England. His enthusiasm for teaching botany made it one of the most popular subjects at Cambridge for several decades. Henslow was also a devout Christian and Anglican clergyman. One of his favorite students and friends was Charles Darwin. On campus, Darwin was known as "the man who walked with Henslow." Darwin learned much about nature from his mentor but he rejected Henslow's faith. When Darwin's *Origin of Species* was published in 1857, Henslow graciously expressed his opposition to the book with the words, "Darwin attempts more than is granted to man, just as people used to account for the origin of evil - a question past finding out."

Walter Lammerts (1904-1996) was the first president of the Creation Research Society. This unique organization began in 1963 for the purpose of promoting the creation worldview. With hundreds of member scientists worldwide, the society encourages the research and publication of creation topics. Lammerts was brought up in Washington and California in an agricultural family. He learned horticulture first hand, and went on to earn a Ph.D.

Geneticist Walter Lammerts introduced new rose varieties including Queen Elizabeth in 1954.

in plant genetics. Lammerts joined the faculty at UCLA and over the years became a world-class expert on rose breeding. He is credited with introducing 46 new rose varieties. Some varieties are given exotic names such as Chrysler Imperial and Queen Elizabeth. Lammerts was bold in his stand for a young earth, a global flood, and the creation of all living things "after their kind," a phrase from Genesis 1. He was a talented scientist who effectively defended God's Word for nearly a century.

Anton van Leeuwenhoek (Leuwenhoek, 1632-1723) was a Dutch scientist who spent years designing and building microscopes. In spite of having no formal optics training, he succeeded in magnifying images as much as 500 times, an achievement unsurpassed until the 1800s. Leeuwenhoek's discovery of bacteria and spermatozoa were described in a published letter which he titled "Observations... concerning Little Animals." He wrote, "In the year 1675 I discovered living creatures in rainwater, which had stood a few days in a new earthen pot." He dedicated much of his life to showing that the spontaneous origin of life was impossible. Leeuwenhoek held a solid Dutch Reformed faith. His writings often refer to the wonder of God's design of creatures, both small and large. Leeuwenhoek's microscope has indeed shown us the beautiful, complex details of nature on an ever smaller scale.

Anton van Leeuwenhoek's early microscopes used water droplets as lenses.

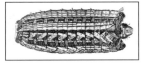

Pierre Lyonnet illustrated caterpillar larva and muscles.

Pierre Lyonnet (1708-1789) was born in the Netherlands. As a pioneer entomologist, he wrote an entire book about the "goat-mouth" caterpillar. His beautiful engravings distinguish more than 4,000 separate muscles, nerves, and membranes in insects. These clear illustrations are classics today. Believing strongly in creation, Lyonnet debated those who promoted the spontaneous origin of life. He saw the chief duty of scientists as "decoders of the mysteries of nature." He believed that the more the natural world was explored, the greater should

be our reverence for the Designer. This approach agrees exactly with Romans 1:20 which declares that intelligent design in nature is obvious. In Lyonnet's view, scientific exploration was one of the most worthwhile tasks for mankind to undertake.

George Mivart (1827-1900) was an English biologist and also a devout Catholic. His comprehensive 1881 text on the anatomy of the household cat, 557 pages long, guided generations of students. Mivart struggled to combine creation and evolution, finally concluding that God had infused a soul into ape-like creatures. Mivart's views were expressed in his books *On the Genesis of Species* (1871) and *Man and Apes* (1873). This position today is called theistic evolution. In Mivart's day, such writing led to his excommunication from the Catholic Church. Although still popular and accepted today by the Vatican, theistic evolution is neither supported by Scripture nor by scientific data. Even with this limited acceptance of God's work in nature, however, Charles Darwin attacked Mivart for "religious bigotry." As is often the case, compromise positions are not satisfactory to either side of the creation-evolution issue.

John Needham (1713-1781) was director of the Royal Academy in Belgium. He did early microscopic work with plant pollen and also with animal tissue. A genus of Australian plants, *Needhama*, is named in his honor. Needham once debated French naturalist Comte de Buffon who believed in a chance, random origin of life. Needham said that God did not allow pure chance in reproduction, but instead predetermined the traits of every human embryo. Needham thus defended the Christian faith against early trends in evolutionary biology. He also debated the French philosopher Voltaire who rejected biblical miracles. Creation-evolution tensions have continued over the centuries. The basic choice is where one places his trust, either in random chance or in the Creator of the universe.

John Needham studied pollen from common plants. Shown here are pollen grains from the sunflower, lily, and morning glory. Each is about the size of the thickness of this page.

Jan Swammerdam (1637-1680) carried out studies of insects which he collected throughout Europe. He believed that they were part of the original creation, no less perfect

Jan Swammerdam made these drawings of mayflies. This insect lives only 1-2 days.

or complex than the "higher" animals. A book Swammerdam wrote in 1675 about the mayfly includes an extended hymn of praise to the Creator. He saw in the brief life of the mayfly, just 1-2 days, a picture of man's own brief existence on earth. As Psalm 90:10 expresses it, our lives are short and we soon "fly away." Swammerdam opposed the idea of the spontaneous generation of life which already was popular three centuries ago. He had seen firsthand the complexity of life, especially in the insect world. He was also the first scientist to study and describe red blood cells in his *Bible of Nature*, written in 1658. This book was unnoticed for decades, and then generated great interest when it was republished in 1737. Some biographers call Swammerdam a religious mystic who was caught up in superstition. However, he clearly saw the world and its life as established supernaturally by the Creator.

Abraham Trembley (1710-1784) from Switzerland is regarded as the father of experimental zoology. His classic book *Memories* (1744) explained the locomotion and regeneration of freshwater organisms called hydra. Trembley also made early studies of stem cells and remarked on their regenerative capacity. Today, centuries later, stem cell research is of major interest. Trembley was a family man who spent much time homeschooling his five children. From this experience he wrote *Instructions from a Father to his Children Concerning Nature and Religion* (1775). Trembley's Christian faith motivated his research into the details of nature. He wrote, "Seen clearly, Nature inspires within us ideas more worthy of the infinite wisdom of its Author and thereby more suitable for shaping our spirits and hearts."

Friedrich von Huene (1875-1969) was a German paleontologist who produced hundreds of original publications. A century ago he did pioneer work on dinosaur fossils found in Patagonia, Argentina. This region of southern Argentina remains an active area for dinosaur discoveries. Von Huene named dozens of dinosaur species. In 1887 he was a major proponent of the division of dinosaurs into the Saurischia and Ornithischia branches. These are respectively the "lizard-hipped" and "bird-hipped" varieties, the classification used today. The son of a Lutheran pastor, von Huene was a deeply religious scientist. He wrote that his research showed the intricacies of divine creation to those with eyes to see.

The fossil of this Aucasaurus dinosaur was found in 1999 in Patagonia, Argentina.

The fossil Archaeopteryx, "ancient flyer," looks similar to some modern birds.

Johann Andreas Wagner (1797-1861) was a German paleontologist who studied the discipline which explores past life on earth. He published numerous works concerning the fossils of fish and reptiles found in Europe. Wagner was a firm believer in biblical creation. When the famous *Archaeopteryx* fossil was reported in 1861, the final year of his life, Wagner argued against its being a transition between reptiles and birds which he called an "adventurous" idea of Charles Darwin. The debate over the significance of Archaeopteryx continues today, a century and a half later. Instead of a missing link, Archaeopteryx appears to be 100 percent bird with bones and feathers designed for flight.

Izaak Walton (1593-1683) is a name which is familiar to those who are serious about fishing. Walton's book, *The Compleat Angler* (1653), popularized the sport and also showed his competence as a zoologist. Both Anglican faith and natural history are integrated throughout Walton's classic book. He was a writer and apologist for the conservative Christian view held by the early Angli-

The front of Izaak Walton's 1653 book Compleat Angler *quotes John 21:3, "Simon Peter said, 'I go fishing'; and they said, 'we also will go with thee.'"*

can Church. Two of his quotes follow. "God has two dwellings: one in heaven, and the other [in] a meek and thankful heart." "Look to your health, and if you have it, praise God and value it next to conscience; for health is a blessing that no mortals are capable of, a blessing money cannot buy." A poem by Izaak Walton reflects on the fishing background of several of the Lord's disciples:

The first men that our Savior dear
Did choose to wait upon Him here;
Blest fishers were; and fish the last
Food was, that He on earth did taste:
I therefore strive to follow those,
Whom He to follow Him hath chose.

Albert Julius Wilhelm Wigand (1821-1886) was a German professor, writer, and botanist. In plant physiology he was a pioneer in microscopic staining techniques. This process reveals details previously unseen on microscope slides. Wigand actively opposed Charles Darwin's evolutionary ideas. In two books on Darwinism, Wigand challenged the spontaneous origin of life and macroscopic evolution. The scientific data from Wigand's microscope studies promoted biblical creation.

Francis Willughby (1635-1672) was a zoologist and a charter member of the Royal Society of London. He was greatly influenced by his creationist professor John Ray at Trinity College in Cambridge. Willughby cataloged many plant and animal specimens, but he assumed that his writings were unworthy of publication. John Ray counseled Francis Willughby that natural history publications were needed as a means of glorifying God. Several books by Willughby then followed, some of them published after his death. Willughby's systematic studies of birds and fish paved the way for modern classification systems.

Chapter 5

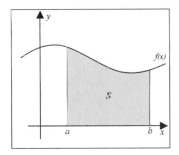

MATHEMATICS

Mathematics is the underlying language of creation. Intricate patterns, symmetries, design, and order exist throughout nature, all revealing the fingerprint of the Creator. Even in a world marred by the Fall of mankind as described in Genesis 3, the details of intelligent design remain clear. To the present day, mathematicians continue to formulate new theorems, equations, and functions. Often, at a later time, these theoretical ideas are found to exactly describe physical phenomena in nature. This trend shows that mathematical structures are embedded in nature, waiting to be discovered. In Albert Einstein's words, "How is it possible that mathematics, a product of human thought that is independent of experience, fits so excellently the objects of physical reality?" Why indeed! The following men and women displayed outstanding mathematical insights, and they acknowledged their discoveries as gifts from the Creator.

Niels Henrik Abel (1802-1829) was born into poverty in Norway. When his pastor father died, 18-year-old Niels Abel cared for his mother and six siblings while studying mathematics during free moments. He soon was making major contributions to trigonometry theory, especially the study of difficult transcendental functions. Abel also founded group theory which remains a major field of research and application today. The class of *abelian* groups are named in his honor. Abel always maintained the Lutheran faith of his youth, and a poor family background did not dispel his optimistic outlook on life. Unfortunately Abel's life was cut short at age twenty-six by a tuberculosis epidemic.

A Norwegian stamp honors mathematician Niels Henrik Abel.

Maria Gaetana Agnesi (an YAY zee, 1718-1799) was one of the most extraordinary women scholars of all time. By the age of 10, this girl from Milan, Italy, had mastered French, Latin, German, Greek, Spanish, and Hebrew languages. The oldest of 21 children from three marriages, Maria followed her father into the world of mathematics. She expanded the known calculus theory of her day, writing *Analytical Institutions* (1748) in two large volumes. Only her womanhood prevented Maria from honored membership in the mathematical societies of her day. Her Catholic faith grew stronger over the years. Around the age of 45 Maria began to devote her time to helping the sick and poor. She took charge of a local hospital and became known as "an angel of consolation" to those in need. Upon her death Maria was buried alongside some of the patients she had cared for. This dear woman combined an outstanding mathematics career with a life of sacrificial Christian service to others.

Maria Agnesi excelled in languages, philosophy and mathematics.

George Boole (1815-1864) was the British mathematician who helped establish symbolic logic, also called Boolean Algebra. Boole was trained as a pastor with a special interest in creation studies. When Boole met someone on a train or in a shop whose conversation interested him, he often invited his new acquaintance to his home to observe stars with his telescope and to discuss current science topics. Boole's binary mathematical abilities were self-taught. His unique algebraic system waited a century until the modern digital electronics revolution to find widespread application. Boole had a great interest in the spiritual welfare of youth. In a sermon to students he said, "Would that some part of the youthful enthusiasm of this present assembly might thus expend itself in labors of benevolence. Would that we could all feel the deep weight and truth of the Divine sentiment that 'no man liveth to himself and no man dieth to himself.'" This truth is taken from Romans 14:7. Boole's final words were the request that his five young daughters not fall into the hands of the liberal preachers of his day.

Decimal	Binary
0	0
1	1
2	10
3	11
4	100
5	101
6	110
7	111
8	1000
9	1001
10	1010

Binary numbers were studied by George Boole 150 years ago.

Georg Cantor (1845-1918) made many contributions to mathematics. As a German professor he explored Fourier Series, set theory, infinite numbers, and logic. Cantor's father was a devout Lutheran and his mother a Roman Catholic. These parents encouraged a religious worldview which Cantor applied to mathematics. He thought deeply of the philosophical concept of infinity. Cantor proved that some mathematical infinities are actually bigger than others. He thus showed that there is a hierarchy of infinities. His title for God was the *Absolute Infinite*. Cantor expressed this view in one of his final letters (Dauben, 1990), "What surpasses all that is finite and transfinite [infinite] is...the single, completely individual unity in which everything is included...incomprehensible to the human understanding...which by many is called God." Cantor saw his theoretical research as a way to harmonize mathematics and faith in the infinite Creator.

Georg Cantor is the father of set theory, a modern branch of mathematics.

Augustin Louis Cauchy (1789-1857) is well known in mathematics history. He did much original work on the solution of differential equations and also the development of group theory. During the final 19 years of his life, Cauchy produced more than 500 technical papers explaining the mathematical foundations of mechanics, physics, and astronomy. He was one of the first to explore the important mathematical concepts of limit and convergence of functions. Brought up in a French Catholic family, Cauchy took this heritage of faith seriously and was very evangelistic toward others. His final words were to the Archbishop of Paris who was at his side, "Men pass away but their deeds abide," a truth found in Romans 2:6.

Augustus DeMorgan (1806-1871) was a world class mathematician who founded symbolic logic along with George Boole. Two centuries later this field of mathematics is essential to the growth of digital electronics and computers. In 1845, DeMorgan suggested the slanted line used for writing fractions, such as ½. DeMorgan was a Christian with strong principles. He was never awarded his graduate degree from Trinity College in England because he refused to sign a questionable doctrinal statement. He called himself both a Britain and a Christian "unattached." A sentence in DeMorgan's will reads: "I commend my future with hope and confidence to Almighty God; to God the Father of our Lord Jesus Christ, whom I believe in my heart to be the Son of God but whom I have not confessed with my lips because in my time such confession has always been the way up in the world."

Leonhard Euler (1707-1783) was born in Switzerland, the son of a Calvinist pastor. One of the greatest mathematicians of all time, Euler always remained close to his Christian roots. Although he became blind in later years, Euler still managed to dictate outstanding mathematics papers and books totaling 70 volumes, long before the days of word processors. He was thus one of the most prolific mathematicians of all time. It is estimated that it would take eight hours of work per day for 50 years to copy all of Euler's mathematical work by hand. He introduced many symbols which fill modern mathematics books including e (the base of natural logarithms), i (imaginary numbers), f[x] (functions), and Σ (summation). Leonhard and his wife Katherine had 13 children, and Euler claimed that their home was his greatest joy. Euler's contemporaries included the French atheists Voltaire and Denis Diderot. Confident in his faith, Euler also enjoyed humor. One day, while in the royal presence of Russia's Catherine the Great, Euler and Diderot debated theology. At one point Euler is said to have challenged Diderot, "Sir, $(a+b^n)/n = x$. Therefore God exists. What is your reply?" Diderot, not realizing that the formula was meaningless, sat in embarrassed silence. The room erupted in laughter and Diderot soon retreated to his home in France (Newman, 1956).

Leonhard Euler was one of the greatest mathematicians of all time. This painting is by Emanuel Handman.

Willem Jacob s'Gravesande (1688-1742) was an outstanding Dutch mathematician. His *Mathematical Elements of Physics* (1720) promoted the creation worldview of his contemporary Isaac Newton. s'Gravesande wrote that the task of physics was to determine the laws of nature as laid down by the Creator, and to unfold their regular operation throughout the universe. Newton entirely agreed with this lofty job description for scientists. s'Gravesande also wrote *Mathematical Elements of Natural Philosophy*, published in 1747.

Charles Hermite (1822-1901) was a French mathematician who became famous for his analysis of elliptic and transcendental functions. At age 34, Hermite experienced an encounter with God during a severe illness with smallpox. At this time his friend Augustin Cauchy encouraged Hermite toward a conservative Roman Catholic faith. Hermite's reputation became one of humility, concern for the welfare of others, and a firm belief in his Creator. In a letter to a friend Hermite wrote, "He who strays from the paths traced by providence [that is, God's will] crashes."

Christiaan Huygens (1629-1695) was Europe's greatest mathematician during his lifetime. He was educated at home with emphases in music, Latin, Greek, French, Italian, and mathematics. His accomplishments include the invention of the pendulum clock in 1656, the pocket watch, many geometry theorems, optics laws, and the discovery of Saturn's largest moon Titan in 1655. Huygens published the first book on probability in 1657, and also developed the wave theory of light. Light is recognized today as having a *dual nature*, acting as both a particle and also as a wave. *Cosmotheoros* ("The Celestial Worlds Discovered") was found after Huygens's death and was published posthumously in 1698. In the book he reasons that God's providence and wisdom are made manifest in the creation and complexity of living and non-living things, including the mystery of light.

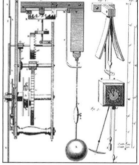

(Top image) Christiaan Huygens wrote the first book on probability theory in 1657. (Bottom image) Pendulum clock drawings by Christiaan Huygens.

Leopold Kronecker (1823-1891) was the son of prosperous Jewish parents in Poland. Kronecker's name today appears often in mathematical physics. For example the Kronecker delta function, used in mathematical physics, is named in his honor. He made important contributions to the theory of algebra, elliptical functions, and also calculus. Kronecker had a special fondness for the beauty of integers which are whole numbers such as 4 or 100. Kronecker once jokingly said, "God made the integers, all else is the work of man." By this statement he paid tribute to the design and elegance of integer numbers. Each of Kronecker's six children embraced the Christian faith. Following their example, Kronecker himself converted from Judaism to evangelical Christianity in the final year of his life at age 68.

Colin Maclaurin (1698-1746) was the son of a Scottish pastor. As an outstanding mathematician, Maclaurin was invited to join the prestigious British Royal Society at the young age of 21. The Maclaurin power series, a special case of the Taylor series, is used universally in modern mathematics to expand functions. Maclaurin held an unwavering belief in God and in the future life. After his death in 1746, Maclaurin's friend Alexander Munro paid tribute to him with these words: "He was more nobly distinguished from the bulk of mankind by the qualities of the heart: His sincere love of God and men, his universal benevolence and unaffected piety together with a warmth and constancy in his friendship that was in a manner peculiar to himself." The Maclaurin Institute is located at the University of Minnesota, Minneapolis, and seeks to carry on Colin Maclaurin's integration of Christian faith and scholarship.

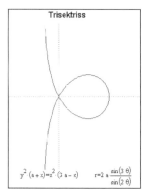

Trisektriss

$$y^2(a+x)=x^2(3a-x) \quad r=2a\frac{\sin(3\theta)}{\sin(2\theta)}$$

Colin Maclaurin explored the details of this trisectrix curve in 1742.

Pierre-Louis de Maupertuis (1698–1759)

distinguished himself in mathematics, physics, and biology. He also was an early president of the French Academy of Science. Maupertuis did initial studies on the principle of least action which describes the tendency of nature to function in the most efficient way possible. For example, a light ray always follows the path of minimum time when traveling between two points. Maupertuis wrote in his 1750 *Essays on Cosmology* that the principle of least action proves the existence of God. In his words, "These [conservation] laws, so beautiful and so simple, are perhaps the only ones which the Creator and Organizer of things has established in matter in order to effect all the phenomena of the visible world." Maupertuis had a deep understanding of the designed, unchanging laws that govern the physical universe.

French mathematician Maupertuis traveled to Lapland in 1736 to measure earth latitudes. Here he wears a fur coat from the northern expedition.

Marin Mersenne (1588-1648)

was a close friend of the creationist astronomer Pierre Gassendi who was introduced in chapter one. Mersenne advanced the study of acoustics, mechanics, and optics. As one example, in 1634 he discovered the well-known law that the period of a pendulum swing varies as the square root of its length. This means a pendulum four feet long swings in exactly twice the time of a one-foot pendulum. Mersenne also described the mathematical details of the cycloid curve. This is the curved path traced out by a point on a circle that rolls in a straight line, such as a bicycle wheel. The technical details of this complicated curve had previously provoked many quarrels

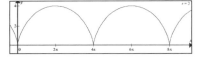

The cycloid is the curve mapped out by a point on a wheel as it rolls.

between mathematicians. A Bible believer, Mersenne's 1623 book *Questions in Genesis* defended Christianity against, in his own words, "atheists, magicians, deists, and suchlike." Mersenne carried on an active correspondence with the leading mathematicians of his day. This activity helped promote mathematics progress in the years before publications and dialogue became common.

John Napier (1550-1617) from Scotland invented logarithms which led to the development of the slide rule, a mechanical calculator which was used through the 1960s. He also pioneered the use of the decimal point to separate a whole number from its fractional part. Napier considered himself more of a theologian than a mathematician (Smith, 1998). In 1593 he published a commentary on the Book of Revelation titled *A Plaine Discovery of the Whole Revelation of St. John*. This book urged Scotland to maintain its biblical heritage during times of social change and scientific progress.

John Napier invented logarithms. They are a component of the slide rule calculator.

Charles Sanders Pierce (1839-1914) made original mathematical contributions in several areas. He studied associative algebra, the theory of aggregates, transfinite arithmetic, and probability theory. Pierce was also interested in the integrity and well being of American society. In an article on mathematical logic called "The Red and the Black," Pierce showed that an optimistic hope for the future is essential for a community's health. After discussing hope, he went on to discuss the importance of charity, or love for others, and also faith in God. Pierce wrote,

It interests me to notice that these three sentiments seem to be pretty much the same as that famous trio of Charity, Faith, and Hope, which, in the estimation of St. Paul, are the finest and greatest of spiritual gifts. Neither the Old nor New Testament is a textbook of the logic of science, but the latter is certainly the highest existing authority in regard to the dispositions of the heart which a man ought to have.

Charles Pierce's biblical reference to faith, hope, and love is found in 1 Corinthians 13:13.

Charles Pierce explored many areas of mathematics. Much of his work remains unpublished.

John Henry Pratt (1809-1871) made early studies of the exact mathematical shape of the earth. Our planet is not quite spherical but slightly pumpkin-shaped due to its rotational motion. Pratt's analysis led to equations for the *oblate spheroid*, a sphere slightly flattened at the poles. Pratt also correctly calculated the earth's radius and the precessional motion of its rotation axis because of the pull of the moon's gravity. The son of missionaries, Pratt spent his life sharing the gospel with others. He believed that science and Scripture were complementary avenues for learning about the Creator. His essay "Scripture and Science Not at Variance" (1856) went through many reprintings. Pratt died of cholera at age 62 while in India. Upon his death in 1871, the British newspaper *Times* wrote that John Pratt was "...one of the ablest theologians and most devoted servants... that England ever sent to India."

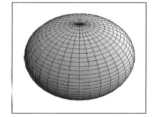

John Pratt determined the exact shape of the earth, called an oblate spheroid.

John Wallis (1616-1703) was a mathematics professor at Oxford University in England. His 1655 book *Arithmetica Infinitorum* ("The Arithmetic of Infinitesimals") contains many original theorems and derivations concerning conic sections. These involve curves such as parabolas and ellipses which often occur in nature. A ball flying through the air and many comets circling the sun follow parabolic paths.

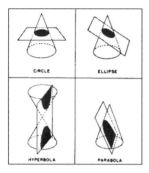

The Wallis book later became a text studied by Isaac Newton. Wallis originated the use of the "lazy eight" symbol for infinity, ∞, in 1657. He also was the first to suggest the scientific law called conservation of momentum, in 1668. This fundamental law concerns interactions between moving objects and is very useful in problem solving. During 1690-1692, Wallis published a series of letters and sermons in support of the Holy Trinity which he directed against Unitarian opponents. As one helpful illustration he compared the mystery of the Trinity to a mathematical cube with its three dimensions of length, width, and height. All three sides equally make up the cube, yet each is distinct. Wallis' lifelong faith was supported by a Puritan upbringing and his membership in the Church of England.

John Wallis studied conic sections which are curves produced by cutting through a cone-shaped solid.

Whittaker had a productive mathematics career at the University of Edinburgh, Scotland.

Edmund Taylor Whittaker (1873-1956) did original mathematics research with differential equations and complex variables. His book *The Calculus of Observations* (1924) was one of the first written expressions of numerical analysis. Thousands of mathematicians worldwide now major in this particular discipline. Whittaker's outstanding lectures at the University of Edinburgh motivated mathematics study for an entire generation of students. Whittaker was a deeply religious Catholic scholar. He wrote that he deplored the trends of modern life in which "the sense of the creatureliness and dependence has passed away, and God is left out of account." Whittaker was a mathematician who also spoke with authority on the theological issues of his day.

Chapter 6

MEDICINE

Centuries ago the inner workings of the human body were a complete mystery. Effective medical treatment was largely limited to herbs and other plants. Ever since the curse of Genesis 3, the world has been subject to disease and suffering. However, pain has been called a "penalty with hope" because great progress also has been made in helping those who suffer. The individuals named in this chapter contributed greatly to the rise of modern medicine. They followed the call to serve the health needs of others.

Jean Astruc (1684-1766) was the chief physician for several dukes and kings in eighteenth century France. Astruc was known widely as a master teacher. He was competent in many areas of medicine and his notes can still be found on file in many medical libraries. Astruc was also an Old Testament scholar, an endeavor encouraged by his Jewish ancestry. His book, *Conjectures on Genesis* (1753), shows that Astruc readily accepted the Bible's inspired accuracy. The Astruc book gives a detailed chronology of Jewish history which is still referenced today.

Drawing of physician
Hermann Boerhaave
(Project Gutenberg).

Hermann Boerhaave (1668-1738) is called the founder of rational medicine and chemistry. During the early 1700s he was as well known as his contemporary Isaac Newton. Boerhaave was the first to isolate the organic compound urea, $CO(NH_2)_2$, and he also pioneered the discipline of physical chemistry. His 1732 *Elements of Chemistry* was translated into many languages and became the standard chemistry text for a century. The son of a Dutch Reformed minister, Boerhaave held strong Christian convictions. He taught that God placed an *aura* in each person at his or her creation which makes us distinct from the animal world. This aura today could be called the human soul.

The British Royal Society,
founded in 1660, is
headquartered in London.

George Cheyne (1671-1743) was a physician and member of the British Royal Society. At age 50 he experienced a spiritual conversion and renounced a rather wild lifestyle, much to everyone's surprise. His reputation took a positive direction from that point forward. His following series of written medical tracts promoted piety and were widely read across England and Europe. Cheyne also studied the abstract concept of gravity. He called this invisible attraction between all objects a testimony to the hand of God in maintaining the stability of the universe. Cheyne's contemporary Isaac Newton totally agreed with this sentiment which remains valid today.

Gravity is indeed a mysterious, invisible glue which maintains planets in their orbits and also holds us on the earth. Regarding the ultimate source of gravity, one is reminded of Colossians 1:17, "He is before all things, and by him all things consist."

Albrecht von Haller (1708-1777) published many anatomical studies, especially those concerning blood circulation. He initiated human anatomy as an experimental science. Haller was the first to show that all nerves lead to the spinal cord and brain. His classic copperplate engravings of the body are still useful today in medicine. Haller also authored the first textbook and laboratory manual on physiology in 1747. During the 1700s there was no easy way to learn the research results of others. To remedy this, Haller compiled a comprehensive list of the scientific writings available in his day totaling 52,000 works. Aside from medical service, this outstanding German scientist is also known as the poet of the Swiss Alps. Haller wrote about the Creator's work in nature:

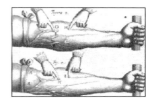

Early blood circulation drawings by Albrecht von Haller.

> *Enough, there is a God, and nature is His script.*
> *The mighty world's whole structure shows his*
> *workmanship.*

Haller saw God's handiwork everywhere, whether inside the human body or across the Swiss countryside.

Friedrich Hoffmann (1660-1742) was an esteemed physician and teacher in Germany. His nine volume series *Systematics of Rational Medicine* introduced the concept of muscle tone as a general measure of health. Muscle tone refers to slight, continuous muscular contractions which maintain posture and balance. Hoffman was one of the first physicians to correctly diagnose many common afflictions including appendicitis (1716), anemia (1730), and rubella (1740). He also was one of the first writers on medical ethics. Hoffmann believed, in agreement with Genesis 1,

Friedrich Hoffmann was a leading German physician.

that God had made mankind entirely distinct from the animal world. Animals are material creatures only, while people receive a spirit or soul from their Creator.

Florence Nightingale promoted careers in nursing (Project Gutenberg).

Florence Nightingale (also Nightengale, 1820-1910) was born in Italy and raised in England. Florence represents many women who pioneered the vital work of nursing. She established schools for nurse training and also wrote 17 medical books. *Notes on Nursing* (1860), the first textbook for nurses, was translated into many languages. In her humility Florence did not consider herself deeply religious. However, she felt that God had directly called her to medical service. Neither her non-supportive family nor marriage proposals altered her path. She wrote, "I am 30, the age at which Christ began his mission. Now no more childish things, no more vain things…Now, Lord, let me think only of thy will" (Coakley, 1990). During the 1853-1856 Crimean War in the Ukraine, Florence endeared herself to injured soldiers. She was known as "the lady with the lamp" since she carried a Grecian lamp while tending injured soldiers through long nights. She also wrote hundreds of letters to the families of soldiers. In Florence's day, most hospitals were dark, depressing places with poor sanitation. Her life's work transformed the image of hospitals to places of comfort, hope, and loving care. There has always been a strong Christian motivation for women in medicine. Other examples from the past include Elizabeth Blackwell (1821-1910) and Elizabeth Garrett (1836-1917), the first women doctors in America and England, and Clara Swain (1834-1910), one of the first female medical missionaries.

Philippus Paracelsus (1493-1541) was the pseudonym or nickname of Theophrastus von Hohenheim. He grew up in Austria and was trained informally in medicine. Paracelsus rejected the outdated traditions of early medicine. Instead he based his treatments on the practical results shown by his patients. He successfully diagnosed and treated miner's sickness, mercury poisoning, goiter, and syphilis. Paracelsus was a man of great faith in his Creator. He believed that God had provided a remedy for every disorder, and that the cures were waiting to be discovered. In his book, *Concerning the Nature of Things*, Paracelsus wrote, "God did not create the planets and stars with the intention that they should dominate man, but that they, like other creatures, should obey and serve him." Paracelsus correctly saw mankind as the capstone of creation, being made a little lower than the angels according to Hebrews 2:7.

Paracelsus is known as the father of toxicology for his work on treatments for poisons.

Ambroise Paré (1509-1590) was a leading French physician known today as the father of modern surgery. He served as chief surgeon for four French monarchs during the sixteenth century. Paré replaced much of the radical, primitive medicine of his day with humane treatment. His efforts greatly increased the survival of patients, especially those with serious military wounds and amputations. For the latter, the traditional treatment was by cauterization with boiling oil to destroy infection and to stop bleeding. Paré replaced the hot oil with soothing ointments. Paré also introduced dentures, artificial limbs, and artificial eyes. For maternity care he pioneered the shifting of difficult fetal positions by gentle abdominal manipulation of the mother. This action has saved countless infant lives during delivery. Paré faithfully prayed for his patients as he treated them. On Paré's statue in Paris is his motto regarding patient care, "I dressed the wound, and God healed it."

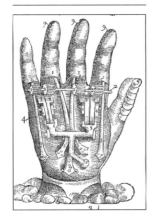

Ambroise Paré worked to relieve military suffering. Shown is his design for a replacement mechanical hand.

Walter Reed (1851-1902) was an outstanding medical officer in the U.S. Army. His bacteriological and viral research helped conquer typhoid and yellow fevers, saving untold thousands of lives. Reed never forgot the Christian up-

Dr. Walter Reed defeated yellow fever by showing its transmission by mosquitoes.

bringing by his Methodist minister father. While stationed in Havana, Cuba, in 1900, his research showed that *Aedes aegypti* mosquitoes were the cause of yellow fever. Military engineers then went to work and eradicated the stagnant water sources where the mosquitoes multiplied. Within 90 days Havana was freed from yellow fever. Reed wrote to his wife, "The prayer that has been mine for twenty years, that I might be permitted in some way or at some time to do something to alleviate human suffering, has been granted." The former Walter Reed Hospital in Washington, D.C., was named in his honor.

The Anopheles mosquito transmits malaria, a medical breakthrough discovered by Ronald Ross.

Ronald Ross (1857-1932) was the first researcher to locate the malarial parasite in the genus *Anopheles* mosquito, in 1897. This discovery showed how malaria was transmitted, and the breakthrough quickly led to widespread control of the disease. "Mosquito brigades" were established in many places to destroy their breeding areas. English physician Ross was also a writer and poet. One of his poems commemorates the finding of the source of malaria:

This day relenting God
Hath placed within my hand
A wondrous thing; and God
Be praised. At his command,
Seeking his secret deeds
With tears and toiling breath,
I find thy cunning seeds,
One million murdering death.
I know this little thing
A myriad men will save,
O Death, where is thy sting?
Thy victory, O Grave?

These final enduring words are found in 1 Corinthians 15:55. Sir Ronald Ross was awarded the 1902 Nobel Prize in Medicine for his work on malaria infections.

Benjamin Rush (1745-1813) pioneered chemistry and medical studies in early America. In 1769 he was appointed to the first U.S. medical college, known today as the University of Pennsylvania School of Medicine in Philadelphia. Rush specialized in diseases of the arterial system, and he also treated mental disorders. While training some 3,000 medical students during his 44-year career, Rush was known as the leading physician in the United States. With the encouragement of his godly mother, Rush had been converted to Christianity at age eight during the first "Great Awakening" revival that swept through the colonies, led by Jonathan Edwards and George Whitefield. Rush remained a devout believer for the rest of his life. He viewed each person as uniquely valuable, existing for special purposes planned by God. Rush was also one of the signers of the Declaration of Independence in 1776 and he attended the Continental Congress Rush pioneered the idea of public schools in America. He wrote in 1787, "Let the children who are sent to those schools be taught to write... [and above] all, let both sexes be carefully instructed in the principles and obligations of the Christian religion. This is the most essential part of education."

(Top image) Dr. Benjamin Rush was converted during a Great Awakening revival. (Bottom image) George Whitefield was a leading preacher during Great Awakening meetings.

Albert Schweitzer (1875- 1965) was a French scholar and musician. At age 30 he felt the call of missions and sought medical training. Schweitzer then spent 50 years in Gabon, Africa. He and his wife Helene treated thousands of patients. They dealt with leprosy and African sleeping sickness, and saw their ministry as a response to Jesus' command to love one's neighbor (Matthew 19:19). Schweitzer was a devout Christian and he readily recognized God as Creator. However, his view of Christ was somewhat unorthodox as described in his 1906 book *The Quest of the Historical Jesus.* Schweitzer's humanitarian work became well-known

An etching of missionary doctor Albert Schweitzer (A.W. Heintzelman).

The Albert Schweitzer hospital in Gabon, formerly called French Equatorial Africa.

This statue in Edinburgh, Scotland, honors Dr. James Young Simpson.

and led to his receiving the Nobel Peace Prize in 1952. When his wife Helene asked Schweitzer how long he planned to stay on the African mission field, he replied, "As long as I draw breath." He died in Gabon at age 90, still at work in his hospital.

James Young Simpson (1811-1870) was a Scottish physician and medical researcher. He was the first to introduce ether and chloroform in 1848 as anesthetics during childbirth, greatly relieving the mother's pain. Simpson wrote *Landmarks in the Struggle between Science and Religion*. This scholarly book shows that historic Christianity is not a hindrance to science. Instead, scientific inquiry and research are encouraged by a biblical worldview. At the close of his life Simpson was asked by a reporter about his greatest discoveries. He is said to have replied, "The greatest discovery I ever made was when I learned Jesus Christ died for my sins." More then 30,000 admirers lined the streets of Edinburgh for Simpson's funeral procession.

Georg Ernst Stahl (1660-1734) was a German chemist and physician who greatly influenced eighteenth-century medicine. He correctly taught that many ailments were then attributed to the wrong causes. Stahl stated that normal blood circulation was essential to maintaining good health. Today it is difficult to realize how revolutionary this idea was. William Harvey had discovered blood circulation in 1628, but its significance was not appreciated for two centuries. The son of a minister, Stahl was a devout Pietist who lived in Europe. He taught that no one can fully explain such details as the extent of the heavens, or why so many different animal species exist in nature. In his view such answers exist only in the mind and will of God.

Nicolaus Steno (also Niels Stenson, 1638-1686) distinguished himself in many fields ranging from geology to anatomy. He made initial studies of the lymph vessels and glands of the human body. Steno also prepared very accurate and useful drawings of the brain, heart, and muscles. A believer all his life, Steno was not impressed with the skeptics of his day. He noticed the scientific errors of philosophers such as Baruch Spinoza (1632-1677) and once told his friend Gottfried Leibniz, "If these gentlemen have been so mistaken with material things which are accessible to the senses, what warranty can they offer that they are not mistaken when they talk [negatively] about God and the soul?" Steno placed all of geologic history within a 6,000-year time span. He is called the father of modern geology for developing rules of interpretation of rock layers. He retired from scientific research in his later years to become an evangelist and missionary for the Catholic faith.

Thomas Sydenham (1624-1689) is known as the English Hippocrates and also the father of English medicine. He was an early founder of clinical medicine and epidemiology, which is the control of disease in populations. Sydenham's book on fevers and epidemics, *Observationes Medicae* ("Medical Observations," 1676) became a standard medical text for two centuries. He was the first physician to study and name scarlet fever, measles, and what is now called Sydenham's chorea. He also led in the use of quinine to treat malaria successfully. This particular drug has given relief and life itself to millions of malaria patients. Sydenham came from an English Puritan family. He trusted in God and believed that the human body had been carefully designed to fight disease. Sydenham was a close friend of Robert Boyle, another strong witness for the Creator.

The Christian Medical and Dental society of Canada takes a quote from Sydenham for its mission statement: "It becomes every person who purposes to give himself to the care of others, seriously to consider the four following things: First, that he must one day give an account to the Supreme Judge of all the lives entrusted to his care. Second, that all his skill and knowledge and energy, as they have been given him by God, so they should be exercised for His glory and the good of mankind, and not for mere gain or ambition.

Third, and not more beautifully than truly, let him reflect that he has undertaken the care of no mean creature; for, in order that he may estimate the value, the greatness of the human race, the only begotten Son of God became himself a man and thus ennobled it with His divine dignity, and far more than this, died to redeem it. And fourth, that the doctor being himself a mortal human being, should be diligent and tender in relieving his suffering patients, inasmuch as he himself must one day be a like sufferer."

Alexei Alexeivich Ukhtomsky (1875-1942) was named for a river in his Russian province. He studied medicine and became an outstanding lecturer on physiology in St. Petersburg. In his day Ukhtomsky was a world expert in understanding the functions of the central nervous system. He belonged to a religious group called the Old Believers, a conservative branch of the Russian Orthodox Church. He openly challenged his students to accept the Christian faith. A man with wide interests including music, Ukhtomsky once gave a talk on "The Splendor of Church Singing" at a 1912 Old Believers' Congress. He died of starvation during the siege of Leningrad in World War II at age 67.

Andreas Vesalius (1514-1564) studied medicine in Europe five centuries ago. He produced several helpful books on human anatomy including *Fabrica* (Full title *On the Fabric of the Human Body*, 1543). Vesalius introduced the use of other languages for medical terminology, especially Latin terms. Many of his choices continue today, such as the names of the three small bones of the mammalian middle ear, the hammer (malleus), anvil (incus), and stirrup (stapes). Vesalius inserted his Christian worldview into *Fabrica* when he wrote, "By not first explaining the bones, anatomists...deter [the student] from a worthy examination of the works of God."

Portrait of Vesalius from his book Fabrica *(1543).*

Selman Abraham Waksman (1888-1973) won the 1952 Nobel Prize in medicine for his discovery of streptomycin in 1944. This antibiotic treats tuberculosis and other bacterial infections. Born in Russia, Waksman immigrated to the United States and worked at Rutgers College in New Jersey and also Woods Hole laboratories in Massachusetts. His research with antibiotics, a word that he coined, greatly relieved human suffering. Antibiotics are substances that kill bacteria without injuring other forms of life. During his career Waksman wrote more than 400 scientific papers and 28 books. His parents grounded Waksman in an understanding of the Bible and the Talmud. He held a lifelong Jewish faith. On his grave in a churchyard in Woods Hole is one of Waksman's quotes, "Out of the earth shall come thy salvation." This is an abbreviated form of a verse from the Apocrypha, "The Lord created medicines out of the earth, and he that is wise shall not abhor them."

Time Magazine *honored physician Selman Waksman on November 7, 1949.*

Chapter 7

PHYSICAL SCIENCE

Physical science includes chemistry, physics, and several related fields. Outstanding physical science creationists of the past include Isaac Newton, Robert Boyle, and Michael Faraday. The additional names included in this chapter are also physical science pioneers. The Christian motivation of their work is seldom included in textbooks today, but their recorded creation testimonies are clear.

André-Marie Ampere (1775-1836) coined the word *electrodynamics* to describe his work with electric circuits and magnetism. He was a child prodigy who mastered the math-

ematics of his day by the age of 12. Ampere's theoretical work earned him recognition from James Clerk Maxwell who called Ampere the "Newton of electricity." Maxwell himself was a world-class scientist and an outspoken creationist. The name of Ampere was commemorated in 1881 when it became the standard unit for expressing electric current, the ampere. Ampere had devout Catholic parents who encouraged his faith. Repelled by the secular French ideas of his country, Ampere challenged skeptics with philosophical arguments proving the existence of the soul and the Creator. Ampere's faith sustained him through domestic tragedy. His father was executed during the French Revolution, and his wife and son also died young.

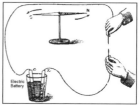

(Top image) André-Marie Ampere explored electricity and magnetism. (Bottom image) Electricity and magnetism were investigated two centuries ago.

Statue of Roger Bacon in the Oxford University Museum.

Roger Bacon (c.1214-1292) was an early English naturalist who promoted the experimental approach to science. This was during the medieval era, three centuries before the time of the better known Francis Bacon (1561-1626), father of the scientific method. Known in his day as the "Admirable Doctor," Roger Bacon advanced the fields of medicine, mathematics, astronomy, and physics. He set the stage for the later invention of microscopes and telescopes through his study of light reflection and refraction. Bacon considered optics a worthy study because light was one of the first of God's creations as stated in Genesis 1:3. Two centuries before Leonardo da Vinci, Roger Bacon proposed flying machines, motorized ships, submarines, and carriages. Bacon was a Franciscan and very loyal to his Christian beliefs. His *Opus Maius* ("Great Work," 1267) argued that theological studies should also encompass the sciences so as to combine special and general revelation, that is, both Scripture and nature. For a time Bacon was imprisoned when he challenged the empty religious rituals of his day. In his day it was dangerous to question such authority.

George Berkeley (1685-1753) was a leading Irish scientist, and at this early date was called a natural philosopher. His *New Theory of Vision* (1709) was the most significant contribution to psychology during the eighteenth century. He challenged those who saw Newtonian science as a mechanistic replacement for God. Isaac Newton himself saw an active role for God in nature, but critics used his newly discovered natural laws to move toward deism and materialism. Berkeley taught that science was composed of a host of principles, which found their unity in God rather than being independent of Him. This reasoning remains valid today. The city of Berkeley, California, is named in honor of George Berkeley.

Portrait of George (Bishop) Berkeley.

Jean-Baptiste Biot (1774-1862) is a name found in texts dealing with electromagnetism. Biot explored many areas of physics including electricity, light polarization, sound waves, and gases. He also showed that meteorites originated in space. Skeptical of the Creator in early life, at age 51 Biot arranged a personal audience with Pope Leo XII. At a later time Biot made a formal return to the Catholic faith of his childhood. His greatest science success followed this spiritual conversion experience. Biot later said that he was greatly influenced by the accomplishments and the testimony of Isaac Newton who had lived a century earlier. Biot wrote, "Words fail to convey the profound impression of astonishment and respect which one experiences in studying the work of this admirable observer of nature."

Samuel Clarke (1675-1729) was a friend of Isaac Newton and held similar interests in physics and natural theology. Clarke presented the Boyle Lectures on these topics in London during 1704-1705. Robert Boyle founded these lectures for defending Christianity "against notorious infidels…" Apparently Boyle was upset with attacks on the inspired Bible. The annual Boyle presentations continue today, although now limited to secular science topics. Clarke's 16 messages were titled "A Demonstration of the Being and Attributes of God." Clarke saw physics principles as evidences of the presence and activity of the Creator. He and Newton were in agreement on God's constant oversight of the universe. Clarke also made major contributions to our understanding of gravity.

Photograph of Danish scientist Ludvig August Colding.

Ludvig August Colding (1815-1888) was a Danish engineer and physicist. He worked alongside the leading physicist, Hans Christian Oersted, in the study of electronics and heat. Colding helped formulate the laws of thermodynamics, especially the law of conservation of energy. In 1852 he measured the conversion of mechanical energy to heat to within three percent accuracy, nearly as precise as similar measurements today. The conservation, or constancy, of energy remains the most fundamental law of nature. Oersted's conservative Christianity greatly influenced Colding in his science endeavors. Colding wrote, "…it was the religious philosophy of life that led me to the concept of the imperishability of forces. By this line I became convinced that just as it is true that the human soul is immortal, so it must also surely be that the forces [laws of nature] are imperishable."

Arthur Compton on a Time Magazine cover, January 13, 1936.

Arthur Compton (1892-1962), born in Wooster, Ohio, received the 1927 Nobel Prize in physics for his studies of x-rays. The Compton effect involves collisions of x-rays with electrons and shows the particle or quantum nature of light. Light has a mysterious, dual nature with both wave and particle properties. Compton was a deeply religious man and described nature in his own words, "Science is the glimpse of God's purpose in nature. The very existence of the amazing world of the atom and radiation points to a purposeful creation, to the idea that there is a God and an intelligent purpose back of everything." When asked to explain the meaning of worship, Compton replied, "A religious observance that is pure and stainless in the sight of God, the Father, is this, to look after orphans and widows in trouble and keep oneself unstained by the world." This good counsel is taken from James 1:27. Arthur Compton and his two scientist brothers Karl and Wilson held an amazing total of 46 university degrees among them. A sister named Mary ran a missionary school in India. Their Presbyterian mother once was asked how she managed to raise such a distinguished family. She laughed and replied, "There wasn't any book to guide me unless it was the Bible."

Farrington Daniels experimented with solar heating and cooking.

Farrington Daniels (1889-1972) led an active career in the physical chemistry department at the University of Wisconsin at Madison. He solved many fundamental problems in nuclear and solar energy. He believed that solar energy was a gift from God with many low-cost applications for the developing countries. Daniels was known as an outstanding university lecturer. During 1953 he served as president of the American Chemical Society. Daniels' life revealed a deep personal faith in Christianity. He applied this faith to social improvement at every opportunity, thus fulfilling the command to love one's neighbor.

Jean Bernard Foucault, French physicist who invented the gyroscope.

Jean Bernard Léon Foucault (1819-1868) was a French physicist with an interest in the properties of light. He designed successful experiments that compared the speeds of light in water and in air. Light travels about one-third slower when passing though water. Foucault also performed a simple and elegant experiment in 1851 that demonstrates the earth's rotational motion. He showed that a pendulum would *precess* in a circle, moving slightly to the right (in the

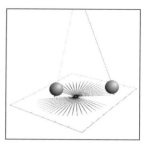

The Foucault pendulum which demonstrates the earth's rotation.

Northern Hemisphere) with each swing. This is because of the earth's turning or rotational motion. Many modern science buildings and museums display a Foucault Pendulum that similarly illustrates the earth's rotation. Foucault also invented gyroscopes that stabilize the flight of modern aircraft and space probes. A nonbeliever most of his life, Foucault finally gave honor to his Creator during an illness, probably multiple sclerosis or Lou Gehrig's Disease, which took his life at age 48. A great physicist of his era, Foucault's name is cast into the ironwork of the Eiffel Tower in Paris.

George Fownes (1815-1849) received the prestigious British Royal Institution prize in chemistry for his many accomplishments. He isolated and identified several new organic chemicals including the useful materials furfural and benzene. Fownes also determined the precise atomic weight of carbon atoms. This was accomplished before the periodic table of elements was constructed. In 1844, he discovered phosphate in igneous rocks and showed how this chemical migrates from eroded rocks and accumulates in clay and soil. One of Fownes' popular essays was titled *Chemistry as Exemplifying the Wisdom and Beneficence of God* (1844). This volume promoted intelligent design based on the chemical composition of the earth, sea, and atmosphere. Fownes saw the various chemical abundances as planned by the Creator for our benefit.

Benjamin Franklin (1706-1790) was a gifted statesman, writer, inventor, and scientist. In 1743 he helped start the American Philosophical Society, similar to Britain's Royal Society. This was the first scientific society in America. Franklin performed his famous kite experiment in 1752, which showed that lightning is a powerful form of static electricity. Around this time he also invented the lightning rod and coined the words "positive" and "negative" to describe the two opposite types of electric charge. Other inventions include bifocals, the odometer, and the Franklin stove.

As a lad, Franklin had been "tithed to the Lord" as the tenth son of his parents. He was trained in the Greek language and in Bible exposition. Franklin composed his own epitaph that shows his belief in the afterlife:

> *The body of*
> *B. Franklin, Printer*
> *(Like the Cover of an Old Book*
> *Its Contents torn Out*
> *And Stript of its Lettering and Gilding)*
> *Lies Here, Food for Worms.*
> *But the Work shall not be Lost;*
> *For it will (as he Believ'd) Appear once More*
> *In a New and More Elegant Edition*
> *Revised and Corrected*
> *By the Author.*

Benjamin Franklin's lightning experiment with his son William (NOAA Photo Library).

Clearly, Franklin had great respect for his Creator. As a deist, Franklin's particular beliefs about the Christian faith are open to question. This was in spite of the strong influence of his close friend, evangelist George Whitefield.

John Hall Gladstone (1827-1902) pioneered the study of optical phenomena in chemistry. He measured the refraction or bending of light in many chemical solutions as a technique to explore their physical properties. Gladstone was a fellow in the Royal Society and also was the first president of the British Physical Society. He remained deeply involved in religious movements throughout his chemistry career. Challenging the trends of his day, Gladstone taught that there was no necessary conflict between Christianity and science. Referring to the Bible opposition he wrote,

The store houses of natural science have often been ransacked for weapons against the old book; the defenders of the faith have sometimes shrieked with alarm, and the assailants have sung their paean in anticipation of victory. Earthworks which form no part of the original fortress have been easily carried, but the citadel itself has remained unshaken and the very vigor of the repeated attacks has proved how impregnable are its valuable walls.

Gladstone supported the British YMCA at a time when the organization was strongly evangelical. He also was active in the Christian Evidence Society and the Victory Institute, two early groups that supported biblical scholarship.

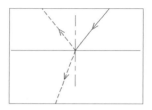

Eight centuries ago, Robert Grosseteste studied the optics laws of reflection and refraction.

Robert Grosseteste (c. 1168-1253) was a central figure in British natural history studies eight centuries ago. At that early date Grosseteste described the optical laws of reflection and refraction. During A.D. 1235-1240, he wrote the text *De luce* ("Concerning light"). Grosseteste saw light as a fundamental part of nature because it was created on the first day of the creation week (Genesis 1:3). He was a teacher of scientist Roger Bacon who is discussed earlier in this chapter. Centuries before Newton, Grosseteste also explained the lunar tides and the detailed motions of the earth that affect the calendar. A man of strong Christian faith, he encouraged the study of the Bible in its original languages of Hebrew and Greek. Grosseteste wrote several useful commentaries on Scripture. A humble man, he refused the academic honors and financial rewards of his day. In 1232 Grosseteste wrote to his sister, "If I am poorer by my own choice, I am made richer in virtues."

Theodore Haak (1605-1690) was a natural philosopher known for originating the Royal Society of London in 1662. He wrote of the need for mankind to improve "the treasures God hath communicated to them so abundantly throughout the world...that they may be willing to listen to more and more and still better Truths." Clearly, Haak saw the need for creation truths to be explored and shared. At this time in history, natural philosophy was generally defined as the study of God's revelation in creation. Haak believed that this study would lead to piety, peace, order, and community among mankind. Over a 12-year period, Haak translated the *Dutch Bible and Annotations* into English. This work came to be called the *Haak Bible*. It is still useful today, four centuries later, as a tool to better understand Dutch vocabulary from past centuries.

Johannes Baptista van Helmont (1579-1644)

was the most important chemist in Europe during the early seventeenth century. He discovered carbon dioxide gas and also helped formulate the law of conservation of matter. He coined the term "gas," the word taken from the Flemish word for chaos, *geist*. Helmont applied chemical principles to physiological problems and became known as the father of biochemistry. Helmont believed that God had established the properties and laws of nature during the literal, supernatural week of Creation. He wrote, "I believe that nature is the command of God, whereby a thing...doth that which it is commanded to do or act. This is a Christian definition taken out of the Holy Scripture." These truths are from Colossians 1:15-17. Helmont was strongly motivated by Christian charity and he freely dispensed medicines to the poor.

J. B. van Helmont saw creation evidence in the world of chemistry.

Victor Francis Hess (1883-1964)

received the physics Nobel Prize in 1936 for his discovery of cosmic rays. These high-energy particles continually arrive from space and interact with the earth's upper atmosphere. Hess' radiation studies involved dangerous balloon ascents to great altitudes. Born in Austria, Hess maintained a conservative Catholic faith. When asked whether scientific progress

Victor Hess made balloon ascents to study cosmic rays (U.S. Navy).

had ruled out biblical miracles, Hess replied, "No, I can see no reason at all why Almighty God, Who created us and all things around us, should not suspend or change - if He finds it wise to do so - the natural, average course of events." Many biblical miracles can be defined as a temporary laying aside of natural laws. The One who established these laws is free to alter them for His purposes.

John Keill (1671-1721) was educated in Edinburgh, Scotland. A personal friend of Isaac Newton, Keill helped Newton defend his physical science ideas against naturalism. Like Newton, Keill strongly believed that science should be subordinate to Scripture. He taught that science would be in error if it left out the important roles played by providence and miracles. This thinking still applies today, three centuries later, particularly in the study of origins and earth history.

Nicolas Malebranche (1638-1715) lived during the reign of France's Louis XIV, also known as Louis the Great. Malebranche is remembered as one of the deepest thinkers that France has ever produced. He made many contributions to philosophy, mathematics, and physical science. He also experimented with the physical laws of energy and momentum. Malebranche maintained a steadfast belief in God as the sustainer of the universe. He taught that a correct knowledge of the world came only by acknowledging the Creator. All across Europe, both friends and critics of Christianity respected the faith of Malebranche, and the grace that he displayed toward others.

Austrian physicist Lise Meitner studied nuclear physics.

Lise Meitner (1878-1968) was a pioneer in nuclear physics studies. Born into a Jewish family, she was one of the first women to earn a doctorate from the University of Vienna, Austria. Lise Meitner performed physics research in Germany until 1938. That year she fled Nazi persecution and immigrated to Sweden where she continued her experimental work on the process of nuclear fission. Element number 109 in the Periodic Table, called Meitnerium (Mt), is named in her honor. Meitnerium was first made in the laboratory in 1982 by fusing together atoms of the smaller elements bismuth and iron. Lise Meitner converted to Christianity as a young adult and joined a group called the Evangelical Congregation of Vienna. Biographer Ruth Sime writes that "she maintained a genuine interest in the ethical teaching of religion all her life."

Dmitri Mendeléev (1834-1907) was the first to organize the atomic elements into the modern periodic table, in 1869. This table somewhat resembles a large calendar with the days of the week replaced by elements. Today this useful table is displayed in many science classrooms and laboratories. One of 17 children, Mendeléev was told by his mother to "patiently search divine and scientific truth." He firmly believed in Scripture, especially Proverbs 25:2 which says, "It is the glory of God to conceal a thing, but the honor of kings is to search out a matter." Mendeléev thus saw chemistry as a royal and godly pursuit. He was led to seek out the underlying order to the atomic elements based on their weights and other properties. In Mendeléev's funeral procession in St. Petersburg, Russia, his appreciative students carried a large banner displaying the periodic table of the elements.

Atomic Number	Electron Configuration
101	2
	8
	18
	32
Md	32
	8
	2
Mendelevium	
[257]	
Atomic Mass	

The element mendelevium in the periodic table is named for Dmitri Mendeléev.

Robert Andrews Millikan (1868-1953) is known for measuring precisely the electrical charge of the electron and also for his studies of the photoelectric effect. This experiment measures the release of electrons when light shines on the surface of metal. The photoelectric effect is the key to many solar energy devices. For his accomplishments Millikan was awarded the physics Nobel Prize in 1923. He also greatly advanced our understanding of cosmic radiation from space. Millikan was the son of a Congregational minister. He often spoke publicly on the subject of science and religion. A firm believer in God, Robert Millikan unfortunately became a proponent of theistic evolution in his later years.

Physicist Robert Millikan at age 23.

Robert Moray (Murrey, Murray, 1608-1673) became the first president of the British Royal Society in 1660. His early studies in metallurgy helped lay the foundation for the worldwide Industrial Revolution. His scientist friend Christiaan Huygens described Moray as the "Soul of the Royal

Society…Religion was the mainspring of his life, and amidst courts and camps he spent many hours a day in devotion" (Merton, 1964). Huygens likewise was a man of Christian faith and a Puritan. The Puritans were a small minority of the English population, yet they made up the majority of those forming the Royal Society. It is clear that experimental science spread rapidly in seventeenth-century England because conservative Christianity encouraged it. There was a strong motivation to explore the details of the designed Creation for the benefit of mankind.

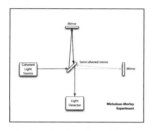

The 1887 Michelson-Morley experiment measured the earth's motion through space.

Edward Morley (1838-1923) is famous for the 1887 Michelson-Morley experiment. This test failed to detect an ether material that was thought to fill all of space. The finding later became an integral part of Einstein's relativity theory that was published in 1905. His Congregational minister father home schooled Morley. He later received training at Andover Theological Seminary in Massachusetts, and pastored a church in Ohio. Morley also had an unusual ability to make precise experimental measurements. He shared this talent with a generation of engineering students at Case Western Reserve Academy in Cleveland, Ohio. Morley's Christian testimony is shown in the creed that he wrote for his students at Case Western: "I believe Jesus Christ shall come with the clouds of heaven to judge the world in righteousness and that those who have believed in Him shall inherit eternal life through the Grace of God."

Henry Morris (1918-2006) was a steadfast pioneer in the modern creation movement. His education was in hydraulics engineering, the study of fluid properties. In 1961, Henry Morris and John Whitcomb coauthored *The Genesis Flood*, which continues to be a best seller. This classic book promotes the biblical, global Flood, and has been an encouragement to many thousands of readers. Morris was a founding member and fellow of the Creation Research Society (see the Life Science entry for Walter Lammerts). He also began the Institute for Creation Research located in San Diego. During his career Morris wrote more than 60 books on Bible-science issues, most of which are still in print.

Thomas Newcomen (1663-1729) is the renowned English inventor of the steam engine. His work was inspired by the need to protect coal and tin miners by removing ground water from their deep pits and shafts. Newcomen's successful engine in 1712 followed years of technical attempts using boilers, pistons, and cylinders. The steam engine remains one of the great inventions of all time because it increased safety and productivity in the workplace worldwide. Newcomen was a leader of the Baptist churches of his region and he preached the gospel to congregations regularly.

The Newcomen steam engine (1712).

Hans Christian Oersted (1777-1851) was a Danish scientist interested in electricity and magnetism. It was during a classroom demonstration in 1820 that he discovered the invisible magnetic field that surrounds a current-carrying wire. From this simple beginning came the entire field of electrodynamics, including the invention of generators and motors. He also discovered pure aluminum metal in 1825 by chemically separating it from earth minerals. Aluminum is the most abundant metal in the earth's crust but is not found naturally in its pure state. Oersted wrote that he was motivated by the belief that "all phenomena are produced by the same original power," a direct reference to the Creator. Oersted taught that we are able to see God in the beauty and unity of nature because we are created in His image.

Max Planck (1858-1947) was the German physicist who originated the modern theory of quantum mechanics. This intriguing field of research shows that atomic particles display wave-like behavior, and light waves likewise act like particles. Planck received the 1918 Nobel Prize in physics for the quantum theory of light. Einstein commented that

Planck's scientific achievements were on a level with those of Isaac Newton. Planck's Jewish family background included a strong devotion to church and state. His uncompromising character earned the respect of other physicists. Planck saw all of science as a pursuit after God. He wrote, "The outside world is something independent from man, something absolute...The scientist seeks by way of inductive reasoning to approach as closely as possible to God and to the order which he has established in the universe." Planck lived a difficult life. His first wife died in 1909, and his twin daughters both died while giving birth. Two sons also perished, one as a soldier in World War I, the other by the Nazis in 1945. Planck's Jewish faith sustained him through these difficult times.

Max Planck was the founder of quantum theory (Courtesy of the Clendening History of Medicine Library).

Some of the gas vessels used by Joseph Priestley two centuries ago.

Joseph Priestley (1733-1804) is famous for his discovery of the element oxygen in 1774. English by birth, Priestley immigrated to the U.S. in 1794 and became America's first prominent chemist. His other discoveries include hydrochloric and sulfuric acids. Like Isaac Newton, Priestly believed that the biblical and laboratory descriptions of nature were closely related. Priestley served as an Anglican minister and mastered the Old Testament Hebrew language. Some of his religious views would be described today as liberal. However he held a confident belief in God and the creation. In his *Institutes of Natural and Revealed Religion* (1782) he wrote, "There never was a time when this great uncaused Being did not exert his perfection, in giving life and happiness to his offspring...The creation, as it had no beginning, so neither has it any bounds."

Leonard Isaac Schiff (1915-1971) wrote the textbook *Quantum_Mechanics* (1949) which is a modern classic in physics. He chaired the physics department at Stanford University in California, and made many research advances in relativity theory and interactions between elementary particles. Schiff adopted the Christian faith while remaining close to his Jewish cultural heritage. His funeral service included a striking reading, which he had chosen from Scripture concerning the importance of faith. The text from Hebrews 11:3 reads, "Through faith we understand that the worlds were framed by the word of God, so that things which are seen were not made of things which do appear." This verse teaches a supernatural *ex nihilo* creation, that is, from nothing, by God's word.

Thomas Sprat (1635-1713) was an early science historian who helped win respect for the newly formed British Royal Society. Sprat knew the fellow scientists of his day and understood their writings. He promoted the Royal Society, explaining that it was formed "to admire the wonderful contrivance of the Creation," so that praises to God "will be more suitable to the Divine Nature than the blind applause of the ignorant." This lofty support of the Royal Society helped it honor the Creator during its early years. In 1667 Sprat wrote a useful book called the *Early History of the Royal Society.*

Alexander Tilloch (1759-1825) began the British *Philosophical Magazine* (1793) which is still published today. This journal quickly came to play a key role in promoting scientific news worldwide. Tilloch was a natural philosopher who succeeded in popularizing science. He was a member of the Sandemanian Church, as was also Michael Faraday. This conservative Christian group, named for one of its leaders, combines biblical faith with a proper scientific outlook. The group reacts against church hierarchy and also against gaining merit to "work one's way into heaven." Founder Robert Sandeman died in colonial American while establishing churches. On Sandeman's tombstone in Danbury, Connecticut, is the epitaph, "That the bare death of Jesus Christ without a thought or deed on the past of man, is sufficient to present the chief of sinners spotless before God." Alexander Tilloch would have agreed with this statement. A small Sandemanian fellowship of believers continues today in England.

Andrew Ure (1778-1857) was a British chemist and member of the Royal Society. He originated the concept of *normality* in describing the concentration of chemical salts. He also invented an apparatus for measuring chemical alkalinity, appropriately called the alkalimeter. Ure was troubled by the evolutionary trends of his day in geology. He wrote *System of Geology* (1829) for the general public in which the biblical account of creation was given priority over naturalistic theories. Ure saw evolution as undermining the basis of religion and morality. This conservative view did not go over well with the more liberal Royal Society members, forcing his eventual resignation from the Society.

An early battery constructed by Alessandro Volta.

Alessandro Volta (1745-1827) came from a humble Italian family, which he once described as "poorer than poor." Volta nevertheless gained an education and excelled in early electronics research. He invented the first battery that came to be called the "voltaic cell." The unit of electric potential today is named in his honor, the "volt." He also originated useful electrical components called capacitors, or condensers. Volta stressed the need to measure physical properties in terms of precise numbers. He lived in Italy as a conservative Catholic and practiced an active faith. At age 70 he wrote out his confession of faith. This statement provides an imposing rebuttal to those who claim that one cannot be a scientist and also a firm believer in the Creator. Volta's productive life demonstrates the successful career of an outstanding creation scientist.

Chapter 8

MISSING PERSONS

The Appendix following this chapter gives 106 addition-
al names of creation leaders including Michael Faraday,
Galileo, Johann Kepler, and Isaac Newton. Some scientists,
however, openly opposed religion, while still others simply
did not publicly express faith in a personal Creator. God
alone knows the inner heart and faith of each man and
woman. We have only the reputations and recorded legacies
left behind when individuals leave this earth. This final
chapter gives brief descriptions of several men and women
from the non-creationist category. In many cases their lives
were spent in a futile search for truth apart from God.

Isaac Asimov (1920-1992) was a biochemist with an unusual talent for writing. He produced more than 500 volumes, most of them on scientific topics. Several of Asimov's books also concerned Bible subjects, including a detailed commentary on the book of Genesis. However, Asimov held a low view of Scripture. That is, he denied such fundamentals as biblical inspiration, the literal account of creation, the existence of the human soul, and the Trinitarian nature of God. During the 1980s he served as president of the American Humanist Association, a group that tends to discount religion as mere superstition. In an interview published in the magazine *Free Inquiry* in 1982, Asimov explained, "Emotionally I am an atheist. I don't have the evidence to prove that God doesn't exist, but I so strongly suspect that he doesn't that I don't want to waste my time." Isaac Asmiov's earthly opportunity to honor his Maker has now expired.

Isaac Asimov in 1965, at age 45. He wrote 500 books and nearly 100,000 letters (Photo by Jay Klein).

Ludwig Boltzmann (1844-1906) was an Austrian physicist who pioneered the study of heat and statistical mechanics. In particular, he explained mathematically the Second Law of Thermodynamics, which states that all things eventually deteriorate and become less ordered. Alternatively, this law states that energy becomes unavailable over time, usually taking the form of unusable heat. Unknown to Boltzmann, this law of degeneration is predicted and described in Psalm 102:26, where even the heavens are said to perish and wear out like a garment. This universal trend toward decay began at the fall, or curse, as described in Genesis 3. Non-acceptance of Boltzmann's ideas by his colleagues eventually led to his depression and suicide at age 62. Strangely, his death was an ultimate expression of the Second Law, which he himself had formulated. Boltzmann's

The gravestone of Ludwig Boltzmann in Vienna, Austria.

will requested that the symbolic mathematical formula representing the Second Law, $\Delta S = k \ln W$, be placed on his tombstone. This unusual epitaph appears today on Boltzmann's grave in Vienna, Austria.

Marie Sklodowska Curie (1867-1934) is perhaps the most prominent woman scientist of the past century. She dedicated her entire life to the study of radioactivity, a word she coined. Marie and her husband Pierre Curie shared the 1903 Nobel Prize in physics for their research on radiation. Marie also was awarded a second Nobel Prize in Chemistry in 1911 for her discovery of the atomic elements radium and polonium. Marie's mother had a deep Roman Catholic faith and spent much time in prayer. However, when Marie was just seven years old her mother contracted tuberculosis and died. Marie's older sister also died of typhus. This embittered the young Marie toward religion, and she received little spiritual encouragement from her father. He was a freethinker, a group that rejects authority in favor of rational inquiry, especially in matters of religion. Freethinkers deny the inspiration of Scripture and recognize no church authority. At a young age Marie made the decision to turn from religion to science for direction in life. Her daughter Eve later wrote that Marie "gave her [daughters] no sort of pious education. She felt herself incapable of teaching them dogmas in which she no longer believed." Marie Curie's career brought great accomplishments, but not the happiness and contentment she desperately sought. Marie died of leukemia at age 67, a result of her close contact with radioactive materials.

(Top image) Marie Curie is one of the few people to win Nobel Prizes in two fields, physics and chemistry. (Bottom image) Marie Curie's research notebooks record her discoveries about radioactivity.

Charles Darwin (1809-1882) was the British naturalist who popularized the evolution theory. He was preceded by his grandfather Erasmus Darwin (1731-1802) who like-

(Top image) Watercolor portrait of Charles Darwin in his twenties (George Richmond).
(Bottom image) When daughter Annie died at age 10, Charles Darwin turned away from God.

wise promoted evolutionary ideas in his writings. Charles Darwin's books, *Origin of Species* (1859) and *The Descent of Man* (1871), were instrumental in moving science away from its biblical roots. Consideration of the supernatural became mere superstition, and the entire science enterprise thereby became impoverished to this very day. True science is the search for knowledge, or truth, which leads directly to the Creator according to Romans 1:20.

Darwin was plagued by an unknown chronic illness much of his life. His family of ten children also knew grief and suffering. The second daughter, Annie, died at age 10, probably from tuberculosis. The youngest child, Charles Waring, died of scarlet fever at age two. In 1876, a daughter-in-law died while giving birth to Darwin's first grandchild. Darwin could not understand why God allowed these events. He wrote, "...disbelief crept over me at a very slow rate, but at last was complete" (Keynes, 2002). Darwin displayed an insufficient understanding of the fall, or curse, upon mankind and all of nature. In later years Darwin still walked his Christian wife Emma to church, but he no longer entered the door to join in worship. There is a popular idea that Darwin renounced the theory of evolution in his final hours. Evidence for such a conversion, however, is lacking. Darwin appears to have remained negative toward Christian faith to the very end of his life.

Thomas Edison (1847-1931) was one of the great experimental scientists of all time. He owned 1,093 U.S. patents, the most ever granted to an individual. His inventions include the phonograph, movie projector, and the filament light bulb. Edison was an agnostic from his youth, refusing to accept the existence of God. He read the skeptical writings of Charles Darwin, Aldous Huxley, and John Tyndall during his formative years. He later claimed, "All Bibles are man-made." When asked what God meant to him, Edison replied, "Not a (profanity) thing." He went on to express his views in *The Columbian* magazine, "I have never seen the slightest scientific proof of the religious theories of heaven and hell, of future life for individuals, or of a personal God" (Josephson, 1959; Wyn, 1981). These quotes rapidly spread around the world and were a disappointment to many admirers of Edison. However, he was simply repeating the message of the anti-religious books from his formative past.

(Left image) This drawing of a light bulb appears in Thomas Edison's 1880 patent.
(Right image) Thomas Edison in his New Jersey laboratory in 1877.

Albert Einstein (1879-1955) came from a family that was culturally Jewish although not religious. His childhood faith was strong, but it was not encouraged at home. Religion was not discussed, nor were Jewish rites practiced in the Einstein household. In his later years Einstein reflected on his loss of faith that occurred at age 12. He wrote in 1946, "Through the reading of popular scientific books I soon reached the conviction that much in the stories of the Bible could not be true" (Schlipp, 1951). Einstein's early exposure to science books clearly directed his lifelong thinking. The books available during Einstein's youth surely included Darwin's *Origin of Species*

Albert Einstein at age 68, photographed by Oren Turner.

(1859). Evolutionary ideas likewise continue to mislead many others to this day. Einstein often referred to God in his speeches and writings, but always in the limited sense of an unknown force or aesthetic principle. He wrote, "It seems to me that the idea of a personal God is an anthropological concept which I cannot take seriously." Einstein was a brilliant thinker, but he apparently lacked the wisdom of knowing his Maker personally.

Stephen Jay Gould (1941-2002) was a strong proponent of evolution. Raised in a Jewish home, he was taught no formal practice of religion by his Marxist father. Gould describes his entrance into paleontology at the age of five upon seeing a T-Rex reconstruction in New York's American Museum of Natural History. Gould held a life-long science position at Harvard University. Where he popularized the concept of punctuated equilibria. This idea attempts to explain the lack of transition fossils by proposing sudden, large-scale changes in plants and animals. Much of Gould's time was spent arguing against creation and intelligent design. In a December 1988 *Life* magazine article he wrote, "We are here because an odd group of fishes had a peculiar fin anatomy that could transform into legs...We may yearn for a higher answer—but none exists."

Halley's Comet, photographed in 1986 (NASA).

Edmund Halley (Edmond, 1656-1743) is famous for his study of comets. He was the first scholar to predict the 1758 appearance of the familiar comet that bears his name, Halley's Comet. This comet approaches the sun and makes its appearance once each generation, with a revolution period of 75-77 years. Halley also made advances in navigational and general astronomy. He helped finance the publication of his friend Isaac Newton's *Principia* in 1687 (Full title, *Mathematical Principles of Natural Philosophy*). Halley was known as a freethinker, a group that did not accept authority, especially in religious matters. Interestingly, in 1688 Halley suggested that the flood of Noah's day could be naturally explained by the very close approach of a comet and its resulting gravity effects on the seas.

Edwin Hubble (1889-1953) is a leading name in space studies. Although gone for a half century, the shadow of Edwin Hubble still dominates the entire field of astronomy. He greatly expanded the known size of the universe in 1925 when he verified that peculiar fuzzy objects in the night sky actually were entire galaxies located in deep space. Hubble also discovered the stellar redshift rule that indicates the expanding nature of the universe. His father was a student of the Bible and his mother faithfully taught Sunday School. However, Edwin Hubble was apparently not a religious man. Neither his own books nor his biographers give any consideration of religious faith or biblical influence beyond childhood. A Hubble quote reveals his doubts about the understanding of man's place in the universe: "The explorations of space end on a note of uncertainty...we measure shadows...we search among ghostly errors of measurement." Upon Hubble's death, by his request, there was no funeral, memorial service, or marked grave. His wish was simply to "disappear from the earth."

Edwin Hubble in 1949 at the Schmidt telescope on Mount Palomar (California Institute of Technology).

Thomas Henry Huxley (1825-1895) made many discoveries in comparative anatomy. He was the first person to call himself an agnostic, a term he coined in 1869 to describe his rejection of religious faith. Darwin's 1859 *Origin of the Species* set Huxley's direction in life. He remarked, "How extremely stupid not to have thought of that [theory] myself." As an energetic spokesman for evolution he became known as "Darwin's bulldog." Upon the death of his infant son, Huxley showed the despair of agnosticism in a letter to a pastor friend: "If wife and child and name and fame were all to be lost to me one after the other...[I still] refuse to put faith in that which does not rest on sufficient evidence."

Pierre Simon de Laplace (1749-1827) was a leading French mathematician and scientist. In astronomy he popularized the nebular origin of the solar system. In this theory the sun and planets formed spontaneously in space from a vast contracting gas cloud. After publishing his origin ideas in *Celestial Mechanics* during 1799-1825, Laplace met with Napoleon Bonaparte in Paris. The em-

Pierre Simon de Laplace, French mathematician and astronomer.

peror remarked, "You have written this book on the system of the universe and have never even mentioned its Creator." The author is said to have replied, "Sir, I...had no need of that hypothesis" (Newman, 1956). Laplace was a confirmed atheist and did his best to remove religious influence from the science of his day. This unsatisfying approach to life is reflected in the final deathbed words attributed to Laplace, "Man follows only phantoms."

Carl Sagan (1934-1996) was a popular writer and spokesman for modern astronomy. Millions worldwide viewed his original television series *Cosmos* in the 1970s. The overall theme was that "The Cosmos is all that is, or ever was, or ever will be." By the word "Cosmos" Sagan referred to physical matter alone, such as atoms. He rejected the existence of God, angels, a spirit world, or any outside intervention by a higher power. In a book also titled *Cosmos* (1980), Sagan wrote, "Was...matter suddenly created from nothing? How does

Carl Sagan with a model of the Mars Viking lander which searched for life on Mars in 1977.

that happen?...We must, of course, ask next where God comes from...Or, if we say that God always existed, why not save a step and conclude that the universe [itself] has always existed?" Consider Sagan's words during his last year on earth, "I would love to believe that when I die I will live again...But as much as I want to believe that, and despite the ancient and worldwide cultural traditions that assert an afterlife, I know of nothing to suggest that it is more than wishful thinking" (Sagan, 1996).

Harlow Shapley (1885-1972) was a leading astronomer who edited the popular book, *Science Ponders Religion* (1960). He began this book with an arrogance that often typifies modern science. Shapely wrote, "In the Beginning was the Word, it has been piously recorded, and I might venture that the word was hydrogen gas." With this sentence Shapley denigrates John 1:1 that beautifully declares Christ's presence at the creation. Shapley clearly lacked a biblical understanding of reality. By definition, natural science alone is inadequate to explain the super-natural origin of the universe.

George Gaylord Simpson (1902-1984) was a leading paleontologist and zoologist of the last century. He grew up in a Presbyterian family, sur-rounded by the created beauty of Colorado. He wrote his autobiography in 1978, titled *Concession to the Improbable*. In it he explains that dur-ing his graduate school years, reading Darwin's *Origin of Species* led him to turn away from an early faith. Simpson went on to a professorship at Columbia University, New York, and also a career of strong opposition to religion. Consider some quotes from his autobiography:

George Gaylord Simpson was a leading paleontologist of the last century (American Museum of Natural History).

[I] ceased to be a Christian at about 12...I be-came more and more critical and increasingly re-alized that practically nothing the preachers throw at you has any likelihood of being true.

Any sensitive person must feel a basically religious awe in the face of the mysteries of life and of the universe, but belief in a god, in a savior, or in a prophet is nonsense.

The process [of evolution] is wholly natural in its operation. This natural process achieves the aspect of purpose without the intervention of a purposer.

There was no anticipation of man's coming. He responds to no plan and fulfills no purpose. He is a unique product of a long unconscious, impersonal, material process that did not have him in mind. He was unplanned.

Such were the words of a professor who mentored an entire generation of biology students at Columbia University.

George Wald (1906-1997) was a career Harvard profes-sor of biology. He won the 1967 Nobel Prize for his research on the physiology and chemistry of the human eye. Wald was convinced that life began spontaneously. He also knew, however, that such an origin is unobservable and statistically impossible. He expressed this in a 1954 *Scientific American* article,

> *Given so much time,*
> *the "impossible" becomes possible,*
> *the possible probable,*
> *and the probable virtually certain.*
> *One only has to wait:*
> *time itself performs the miracles.*

This argument is not convincing. With or without eons of time, the spontaneous origin of life cannot occur. Time is not the key to miracles as George Wald asserts. Instead, the Creator of the universe is the only miracle worker needed. Dr. Wald gave a famous speech in 1970 titled the *Origin of Death*. In it he claimed that the only form of immortality possible for mankind was the genetic information that we pass on to future generations.

Alfred Russel Wallace (1823-1913) is known as the "other man" who originated evolutionary ideas contemporaneously with Charles Darwin. The parents of Wallace held to the early conservative Christian faith of the Church of England. Wallace completely rejected this family heritage and instead delved into such extreme areas as phrenology, psychic phenomena, and the occult. Wallace believed that through science progress, "We shall be better fitted to enter upon and enjoy whatever new state of being the future may have in store for us." Science has indeed made many discoveries. An understanding of the origin of life and its ultimate purpose, however, requires recognition of our Creator.

Photograph of Alfred Russel Wallace in 1862.

Conclusion

Our brief visit with many pioneer explorers of creation is now complete. Aside from those in chapter 8, each man and woman was a competent, confident witness for the Creator. Today, their discoveries are taught in many books and classrooms. However, the biblical worldview that motivated their scholarly achievements is seldom mentioned. One can only speculate the extent to which the science enterprise has impoverished itself by largely abandoning its foundation. But all is not gloom. Included in the next generation of scientists and mathematicians are many students of faith. They will join the parade of godly men and women who have studied and honored God's Creation across the centuries.

Appendix

*The following is an alphabetical list of additional creation-
ist scientists. They are discussed in the book* Men of Science Men of God *(1982) written by Dr. Henry Morris.*

Abney, Sir William

Agassiz, Louis

Anderson, Thomas

Babbage, Charles

Bacon, Francis

Barrow, Isaac

Barton, Benjamin

Bell, Charles

Boyle, Robert

Brahe, Tycho

Brander,Gustavus

Brewster, David

Buckland, William

Burnet, Thomas

Carver, George Washington

Chalmers, Thomas

Charleton, Walter

Copernicus, Nicholas

Cuvier, Georges

Da Vinci, Leonardo

Dalton, John

Dana, James

Davies, L. Merson

Davy, Humphrey

Dawson, John William

Deluc, Jean

Derham, William

Dewar, Douglas

Dwight, Timothy

Edwards, Jonathan

Fabre, Henri

Faraday, Michael

Flamsteed, John

Fleming, John Ambrose

Galilei, Galileo

Gilbert, Joseph Henry

Glaisher, James

Gosse, Philip H.

Grew, Nehemiah

Harris, John

Harvey, William

Henry, Joseph

Herschel, John

Herschel, William

Hitchcock, Edward

Hooke, Robert

Huggins, Sir William

Hutchinson, John

Huygens, Christiaan

Joule, James

Kelly, Howard A.

Kepler, Johann

Kidd, John

Kirby, William

Kircher, Athanasius

Kirwan, Richard

Leibnitz, Gottfried Wilhelm

Lemoine, Paul

Linneaus, Carolus

Lister, Joseph

MacAlister, Alexander

Mather, Cotton

Mather, Increase

Maunder, Edward H.

Maury, Matthew

Maxwell, Joseph Clerk

Mendel, Gregory

Miller, Samuel

Morse, Jedidiah

Morse, Samuel F. B.

Murray, John

Newton, Isaac

Owen, Richard

Parkinson, James

Pascal, Blaise

Pasteur, Louis

Pettigrew, John

Petty, William

Prout, William

Ramsay, William Mitchell

Rawlinson, Henry

Ray, John

Riemann, Bernhard

Rogers, Henry

Roget, Peter Mark

Romanes, George

Sayce, Archibald Henry

Sedgwick, Adam

Short, A. Rendle

Silliman, Benjamin

Simpson, James

Smyth, Charles Piazzi

Steno, Nicolaus

Stewart, Balfour

Stine, Charles

Stokes, George

Strutt, John

Tait, Peter Guthrie

Thompson, William

Virchow, Rudolph

Von Braun, Wernher

Wakeley, Cecil

Whewell, William

Whiston, William

Wilkins, John

Woodward, John

References

In several cases, final brackets indicate the person referenced.

Bailey, Solon. 1922. "Henrietta Swan Leavitt Obituary," *Popular Astronomy,* 30(4):197-199. Also, "History and Work of Harvard College Observatory," *Harvard Observatory Monograph* No. 4 (New York: McGraw Hill, 1931).

Baker, J. 1952. *Abraham Trembley of Geneva* (London: Edward Arnold).

Barrow, John D. and Frank J. Tipler. 1986. *The Anthropic Cosmological Principle* (New York: Oxford University Press).

Bell, E.T. 1937. *Men of Mathematics* (New York: Simon and Schuster).

Bodanis, David. 2000. *E=mc²* (New York: Walker and Co.).

Bolton, Sarah K. 1977. *Famous Men of Science* (New York: Thomas Y. Crowell Co.).

Bynum, W.F. 2002. "Mosquitos Bite More than Once," *Science* 295:47-48 [Richard Ross].

Christianson, Gale. 1995. *Edwin Hubble, Mariner of the Nebulae* (New York: Farrar, Straus and Giroux).

Coakley, Mary Lewis. 1990. "The Faith Behind The Famous: Florence Nightingale," *Christian History* 9(1):37-40.

Daintith, John, Sarah Witchell, and Elizabeth Tootill, Editors. 1981. *A Biographical Encyclopedia of Scientists* (New York: Facts on File, Inc.).

Dauben, Joseph. 1990. *Georg Cantor: His Mathematics and Philosophy of the Infinite* (Princeton: University Press).

Farlow, James O. and M.K. Brett-Surman, Editors. 1997. *The Complete Dinosaur* (Bloomington, Ind. Indiana University Press).

Gillispie, Charles C., Editor. 1970. *Dictionary of Scientific Biography* in twenty volumes (New York: Charles Scribner's Sons). This source was used extensively.

Gormley, Beatrice. 1995. *Maria Mitchell: The Soul of an Astronomer* (Grand Rapids: William B. Eerdmans Pub. Co.).

Graves, Dan. 1996. *Scientists of Faith* (Grand Rapids: Kregel Resources).

Heeren, Fred. 1995. *Show Me God* (Wheeling, Ill.: Searchlight Publications).

Hellemans, Alexander and Bryan Bunch. 1988. *The Timetables of Science* (New York: Simon and Schuster Inc.).

Howey, Walter, Editor. 1948. *The Faith of Great Scientists* (New York: Hearst).

Jardine, L. 2000. *Ingenious Pursuits* (New York: Anchor Books).

Josephson, Matthew. 1959, *Edison: A Biography* (New York: John Wiley and Sons, Inc.).

Kaiser, Christopher. 1991. *Creation and the History of Science* (Grand Rapids: William B. Eerdmans Publishing Co.).

Keynes, Randal. 2002. *Darwin, His Daughter and Human Evolution* (New York: Riverhead Books).

Larson, Edward and Larry Witham. 1999. "Scientists and Religion in America," *Scientific American* 281(3):88-93.

Mackenzie, W. M. 1905. *Hugh Miller: A Critical Study* (London: Hodder and Soughton).

McHenry, Robert, Editor. 1992. *The New Encyclopedia Britannica* in 29 volumes (Chicago: Encyclopedia Britannica, Inc.).

Merton, Robert K. 1964. "Puritanism, Pietism and Science," *Science and Ideas,* edited by A.B. Arons and A.M. Bork, (Englewood Cliffs. N.J.: Prentice-Hall, Inc.) [Robert Moray].

Milner, Richard. 1990. *The Encyclopedia of Evolution* (New York: Facts on File).

Morris, Henry. 1982. *Men of Science Men of God* (Green Forest, Ark.: Master Books).

Newman, James R, Editor. 1956. *The World of Mathematics* in four volumes (New York: Simon and Schuster) [Pierre Simon Laplace].

Oeland, Glenn. 2001. "William Bartram" *National Geographic* 199(3):104-123.

Osen, Lynn M. 1974. *Women in Mathematics* (Cambridge, Mass.: The MIT Press).

Rigden, John S. 1996. *Macmillan Encyclopedia of Physics* in four volumes (New York: Simon and Schuster).

Sagan, Carl. 1996. "In the Valley of the Shadow," *Parade Magazine* March 10.

Schlipp, Paul, Editor. 1951. *Albert Einstein: Philosopher-Scientist*, Volume 1 (New York: Harper and Brothers).

Shapley, Harlow, Editor. 1960. *Science Ponders Religion* (New York: Appleton–Century–Crofts, Inc.).

Sime, Ruth. 1996. *Lise Meitner: A Life in Physics* (Berkeley: University of California Press).

Sobel, Dava. 1995. *Longitude* (New York: Walker and Company) [John Harrison].

Stephen, Leslie and Sidney Lee, Editors. 1968. *The Dictionary of National Biography* in 22 volumes (New York: Oxford University Press).

Wald, George. 1954. "The Origin of Life," *Scientific American*, 191(2):44-53.

Williams, Emmett. 1996. "In Memoriam-Walter E. Lammerts," *Creation Research Society Quarterly* 33(2):79.

Williams, Trevor, Editor. 1969. *A Biographical Dictionary of Scientists* (New York: John Wiley and Sons).

Wright, Louis B. 1970. *Gold, Glory, and the Gospel* (New York: Atheneum).

Wyn, Wachhorst. 1981. *Thomas Alva Edison* (Cambridge, Mass.: MIT Press).

Scripture Index

Name Index

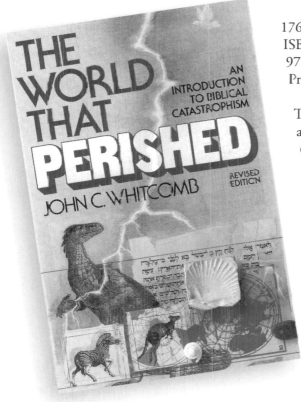

Additional Resource on Biblical Creationism

THE EARLY EARTH

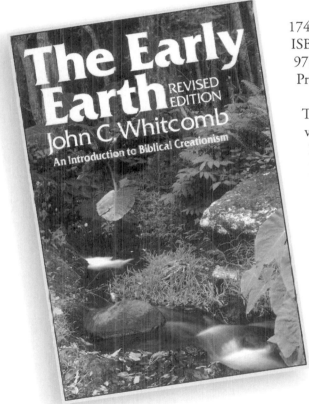

174 pages, Paperback
ISBN: 0-80109-679-0
978-0-80109-679-2
Price: $18.00

This is a companion volume to *The World That Perished.* It provides a special defense of the 24-hour creation days, creation with an appearance of maturity, and a critique of the "Gap Theory" of Genesis 1:1-2.